Progressive Overload

How to Grab
a Shovel
& Start Digging Out

Giovannelli Franchesco, MBA, SGT

outskirts
press

Dedicated to my stepfather. When he died it reaffirmed to me that I couldn't wait to do the things that I wanted to do. I couldn't put my life on standby or "what if." He was fifty-four at the time, and two months before his  *fifty-fifth birthday, he never met his grandchildren and died of cancer. I last spoke to him on February 25th, 2012, not knowing he would give his last breath two days later. He died with an entourage of people all telling the stories of heroism and humility he displayed at every turn. In recollecting all that I witnessed of him, I realized his time with us was short. He somehow had survived many accidents that were supposed to be fatal. Yet, every time he came back, he would tell me and Mom, "I had to come back. You guys were waiting for me and I couldn't go yet." Thank you for holding out as long as you did…to the forgotten Prince…*

Table of Contents

Preface i
CHAPTER 1 1
Here & Now 1
If you can't change what's out, then change
what's within 4
New challenges require a different you 9
Just Do It, there are no in-between, no gray
areas. Just Do It 11
Success requires sweat, pain, and a lot of
bruising…or does it? 13
CHAPTER 2 16
Believe It to Be Possible 16
The Best or Nothing 20
The Reactive Mind vs. the Thinking Mind 24
Of Being a Husband x2…soon to be x3 30
Of Being a Father or a Mentor 36
Of Being a Son 40
What will you do with What Happens to You? . 44
CHAPTER 3 47
Accept the reality before you, or change it 47
The hardest decisions are not always easy 49
The universe conspires to give you what you
want; you just have to ask for it 52
Of Broken Pride 53
Breakthrough 59

CHAPTER 4 63
    Forging an Unstoppable Attitude 63
    Reprogramming the Operating System 65
    Are you worth it? 70
    How to get the fight back in you 79
    On Self-improvement 86
CHAPTER 5 97
    On Acceptance 97
    Efforts 106
    Fight the Fight 111
    The Fight Never Stops, It Just Changes 114
    With Wisdom, you realize the fight was never a
    fight 121
CHAPTER 6 123
    Timed Success…The Clock is Ticking 123
    $$ Money, Money, Maaa...noey $$...! 126
    Abracadabra 128
    Play Time 133
    Desire 136
    The Walkabout 138
CHAPTER 7 143
    Knowing thyself 143
    Hacking the pirate's Map 149
    Air & Water 156
CHAPTER 8 158
    When In Rome 158
    Resolve to Live as a Grown-Up 163
    The Inventory 166

Preface

HUMANS HAVE AN innate desire to aspire. The heights of what humanity can achieve is yet to be discovered, yet to be remembered. Our greatness is asleep, and to awaken it, it takes joy, creativity, passion, love, and in many instances…pain. We defy and protest in spite of the odds stacked up against us. It is never too late to have and be what you want. It looks different for everyone. Not everyone wants what you want. Just ask for it, write it down, home in on it like there is nothing else around you, and you will achieve it. The simple fact that you are human makes you unstoppable. My son taught me many things, but mainly drew out my desire to protect, to fight, to stand firm, and to love. In my journey, I had to drop my addiction to my own self-imposed complexities. I held onto these complexities like pets, and like a good trained dog, they protected me from anything that would be good for me. It took me many years to realize this, to learn coping skills, and to forgive those who hurt me and stepped on me.

It all matters, it makes you stronger; it tests your mettle and forges you into what you truly want to become. You, like I, have to realize your right to command your life. Don't wonder if you can, because if you wonder, someone else will take your place and command your life as they see fit. Through the years I realized that I am not the only one who knows that humans don't just exist for mere existence. We live to reach higher and live happier, to engage, create, ingest, digest, and breathe life. You wield the power to create your own life, to live in abundance; what you want, wants you. Don't wait for catastrophes to occur to take action. Take action now. This is dedicated to all, not just the men and women who stand alone. It is dedicated to the "gladiator." To those who fight for causes bigger than themselves; to fathers and mothers, to those who owe it to themselves to get up when there's nothing to get up for, and those who make it happen every day. You're only aware of the reality you choose to observe, so observe and engage in the reality that fulfills you. Choose to live your life by design, not by default. Remember that death comes to us all, and what you choose to do with what you have is entirely up to you.

As you read, it is encouraged to study the concepts, underline areas where they are of interest to you, and re-read sections. This book was written in hopes that you treat it like a map, and like any good map, it is used to re-examine and to re-route your routines. If need be, disagree with it. If it leads to you question your current path or to improve, it has served its purpose. This book is not meant to be in pristine condition; keep in your pocket, your purse; allow the pages to hang on by their threads.

Disclaimer:

The information in this book is meant to supplement, not replace, medical advice of physicians and/or current professional help. The author and publisher advise readers to take full responsibility for their safety and mental health and know their limits. Although the author and publisher have made every effort to ensure that the information in this book was correct at press time, the author and publisher do not assume and hereby disclaim any liability to any party for any loss, damage, or disruption caused by error or omissions, whether such errors or omissions result from negligence, accident, or any other cause. I have tried to recreate events, locales, and conversations from my memories of them. In order to maintain people's anonymity and to protect their privacy, in some instances I have changed names and places. Giovannelli Franchesco is a pseudonym.

CHAPTER 1

Here & Now

AN IMMIGRANT WITH cultural shock, language barriers, multiple marriages, divorces, a traumatic court battle, single father, addictions, financial issues, and deaths—you don't have to go through these events or reinvent the wheel. Here you will learn a skill set that will set you apart far from the average. But, as it turns out, nothing is free. Yes, you will have to study the book, and yes, you will have to work on "your stuff." If you are ready, tired of feeling defeated, tired of spinning your wheels and feeling like you're getting nowhere, then congratulations! You picking this up is an indication that you are seeking more for yourself. Take control of your life now, and don't live by default. Design your life, visualize your life, and then begin and execute your plan. Life hasn't always been easy, and it wouldn't have been easier even if I had another life. Realize this about your life, and start working with what you have now…here and now!

I could give you the "gold nuggets" in just a few pages, but as it turns out humans love tragedy and drama. They love to see their heroes rise and fall. This is what gives them meaning and motivation. This is what makes them unique. Take heed of the stories, as they are all real, and it doesn't take a celebrity or a millionaire to tell you what you can do to raise your head above the water and succeed. Heroes are everywhere—teachers, construction workers, peace officers, janitors— be your own hero. We all rise and fall; how and when we choose to is our only privilege, our very own right of control. Own this privilege and stop victimizing your life.

*When your mind is where it needs to be,
it finds answers, it creates opportunity
where there is none, and it points out
details you would have otherwise missed.*

We have the choice to adjust along the way, change the "programming" per se, and re-route our conditions to acquire the necessary outcomes we desire.

I have been on a quest for self-improvement, and that has not always been without its bumps. You will find that people give up not due to lack of desire, but lack of belief. The lack of belief is one of the bumps we encounter. The message is simple: don't wait to achieve and do what you have always wanted to do. This is the most basic message I am urging you to receive today.

The most fundamental question, once you have decided to pursue your dreams, is *What now? Where do I go, who do I ask, what do I read, and what do I do?* I will leave you with gold nuggets of information. In the end, however, it will be up to you to decide what you can take away from this, what you find useful, and how you will apply this. Not everyone's life is the same, and although we can definitely share similar experiences, we don't always take away the same lessons. Some people will continue to make excuses for themselves and say that they weren't able to accomplish this or that because they weren't the same as other people who could. Remember, we all have the same twenty-four hours in a day as everyone else. While it is true that some people have advantages in resources, it is still up to you to become resourceful.

Let me be clear, I am not a millionaire, and though I am not necessarily set on being one, your journey can be about being one. What this is really about is developing mental fortitude and strength of character; it's about becoming and transforming into the best version of yourself. In the process of designing yourself, you'll become financially stable, wealthy, or content. Understanding and working on your core will give you the necessary tools to live and pursue a worthwhile dream, and at the very least it will help you be at peace with yourself, something money can't buy.

If you can't change what's out, then change what's within

I'm going to give it to you straight. In this new age of fast digital consumption, no one wants to know the long, drawn-out details. They want it fast, easy to digest, just "the meat and potatoes." There are ten things you should keep in mind. I will go through each one, giving you why it works, how it worked for me, and why it will work for you. You can try to re-invent the wheel, but why bother when I have gone through forty years of sweat, pain, and redundancy to serve it all to you in a neat little package. Isn't this what we all want? After all we all ask, "Why not me?"—the age-old self-reflective questions that make us doubt our own worth, and our same old "it's not fair," "why him and not me" questions.

Well, here it is. No need to wait anymore. Death is inevitable, and it'll come to us all. The real question is whether you will face it with regret or ridiculous optimism derived from your dedicated and consistent habit of "doing you," of taking your goals, your dreams, and your limits just outside of your comfort zones and then taking yourself to the next level. Are you ready? Are you ready to meet the best version of yourself? But will you sacrifice the current you to meet this person? Will you cut out the garbage? Will you cut out the things, places, and people that serve you no good? Will you have the courage to believe in yourself? Someone has to. No one has more right over saving you than you.

Hopefully now you've had enough and are ready to listen and take action. I'm going to drive it home and take it to your doorstep. Glass ceilings, cultural shock, cultural change, language barriers, they all matter because they will all slow you down. It is the catalyst of what needs to change. It's adaptation and evolution at their best. All of what you think is you needs to be changed. Now "change" is a bit of a strong word. So if it is easier to swallow, think of this as habits. Just change the habits. This changes your internal programming, your language, how you think of yourself, and ultimately your self-worth. This gain in confidence will increase your belief system, and you will achieve. You've convinced yourself of that. But you cannot charge like a blind bull. You have to be methodical about what habits you change; you have to think about what you want to accomplish, and why. Most of us have it already, we already know deep inside. So begin to explore this, and inventory what doesn't serve you. Take out the garbage, and take your life seriously.

Being an immigrant, having little to no fluency in the language and very little working knowledge of the culture and the legal system, and with limited support, it was not just hard for me; at times it felt impossible. To add insult to injury, I was raised in a single family household (biological father absent) and poor. Obviously with those challenges it would be too difficult to change those things that are out of my control, or those things outside of me. So if you can't change what is outside, then you have to start with what's within. This journey of course was among my most difficult ones. I was made aware that my existence was conditional, that it was just as dependent upon other factors as it was conditional on me. I knew that part of coming to this country would require me to change, to adapt, to be part of this new world. My old ways would not cut it anymore, that much I knew. The challenges that were before me required a different me; a me that needed to rise above my former self. I needed to shed that person, but how?

In the process of understanding all of this, I came across people who were in similar situations. Some would see the world negatively, in a prejudiced way; one would say that they were seeing the world with the "glass half empty"; and in some situations they would see their world as limiting. Meaning they would see that the access to freedom and abundance were real things, but only granted to a select few, of which they were not a part of. Our perspective is something inside of us, within our control; it's about seeing what's in front of you from outside the box. But in order to build this confidence of seeing the world from outside the box, it's imperative to begin to see the world with the glass half full. The funny thing is that you don't have to be an immigrant to see this. Just look around!

Let me be more specific. You have to be preju- diced in guarding your thoughts, in guarding a positive mental attitude. By this I don't mean that you have to see the world with rainbows and unicorns, although if it helps by all means. It's about establishing mental dominance over your "old brain," over your insecurities, and over your exaggerated perception of negativism. Naysaying only opens you up to possibilities of naysaying. So as a result, you only see the "nay" in every as- pect of your dreams, goals, pursuits, and overall life.

For starters, you have to change aspects of what influences you the most; and most often it's our environment. In many cases it's too challenging to change all of our environment, so we do it one step at a time, starting with what we are in control of, ourselves. Then you branch out to what is im- mediately in front of us, of what we can change. Assess who you associate with, what's around you, and what you see every day; for what you see has to inspire you. Going after what you want means you'll have to give up the "the small stuff." The small stuff that comforts you, the small stuff that consoles your self-pity and your inside voice that convinces you of your "less than" worth. Give that up. It serves no purpose and only enslaves you.

New challenges require a different you

So how does one change? As an immigrant I had to change what I wore, how I walked, and how I spoke. Why? you may ask. Because somehow it mattered; I didn't know why it mattered at the time, or how it mattered, but I knew that it did. I learned that you were treated better by the way you spoke. You were also treated better by the way you dressed. But that wasn't enough. People knew you were different by merely watching how you walked into a room. We can all agree that based on the culture, society rules, or country you live in, things may change. As you acclimate to your new surroundings, you will be more accepted based on how accurate or adept you are at adopting the new culture. The funny thing is, you don't have to be an immigrant to decide to change your circumstances. You just have to decide on it and take action.

I had noticed in that time how everything flowed for my stepfather (whom I will refer to as Dad):

his income, success, and generally speaking everything he wanted. He was an immigrant from Poland, of German/Lithuanian descent. Every time he walked into a room, he commanded respect, and everyone stopped to look at him, to admire him. His face and demeanor conveyed safety and assurance. He was fit, slim, and was always asked for an autograph. You felt safe and empowered around him. He wore his best no matter where he went, what he was doing, or whom he was with. From grocery shopping to cooking, he was always in a suit and tie. But he wasn't always like this. He too had to train himself, educate himself, and practice. When you first meet prodigies, it seems like it's easy for them and that they've always somehow possessed this mysterious power, but under closer observation all if not most prodigies are trained. My dad was no different. In fact he had grown up in a world where he was judged and beaten for his heritage. His father was of Lithuanian decedents and mother of Polish parents. Was it his fault he wasn't born of pure, privileged bloodlines? Nevertheless, he didn't allow that to stop him. It was difficult to get any stories from him of his past. His usual answer was "Giovannelli, we are here and now; the past is gone." I wish he could have told me more, for the sake of wisdom. But there was wisdom in the "here and now." Begin to train yourself in the "here and now." Don't get caught up with the usual BS that attempts to excuse and justify why you aren't at your potential. With time, dedication, and practice, you too will be a prodigy, and everything will eventually seem natural with flow.

Just Do It, there are no in-between, no gray areas. Just Do It

When I'd ask my stepfather about his success, he'd simply say to me, "Just do it. There are no in-between, no gray areas. Just do it." This was as enigmatic as my geometry class. I'd scratch my head while he asked, "You understand, right?" I'd nod in a confused manner. What he neglected to say is that it requires more than a mere "just do it"; it also requires focused attention. Only then can you "just do it." Otherwise you'd be a mindless hammer, hammering at anything that sticks out. Years later during my undergraduate studies, I was taking an economics class where I was introduced to a concept called *geometric progression*—basically, the progression of the last action leading to a faster and stronger action, like a domino effect. So let me back up a bit.

In 1983, Lorne Whitehead wrote in the *American Journal of Physics* how a domino could not only knock down dominoes its own size, but topple bigger things, as big as 50 percent larger. He constructed an experiment where one domino would knock down another domino larger than itself, subsequently knocking down another bigger than the last. Seemingly, an action too small to notice can cause big, huge impacts too fast and too loud to ignore. Why this reference? Because once you are single-minded on a task and you get off your butt and "just do it," you then begin flickering that small domino too small to notice, and eventually too loud and too fast to ignore; in other words, your success.

Every effort you make toward your goal, you're not only building momentum, but a geometric progression. This revelation comes at a cost, however. It is a perishable skill until it becomes a habit. Some people, many of whom you know, get tired of building these habits, because let's face it; performing new tasks is draining if they are not already habits. So in order to get to a point where your small domino flickers become big and unstoppable, you have to keep a positive mental attitude toward every task/action you are trying to create into a habit.

Fast-forward ten years. I was finally able to figure out what the hell my dad was talking about. If your attitude is right, you can program your mind, or will yourself to accomplish anything—from simple tasks like getting up when you feel like you can't, to shaking off fear at an interview.

Success requires sweat, pain, and a lot of bruising...or does it?

So how does this geometric progression work? I had joined Taekwondo early in my teenage years. Little did I know that mastery of skill required sweat, pain, and a lot of bruising. For the first three months, I probably only made it to half the classes. I would tell my parents that I was going, but what I was really doing was going to the park and smoking. Yeah, I know, shame on me. But as any start of a new habit, I found myself starting to attend more and more classes. Finally, at the end of the third month, I tested for my yellow belt. By the end of the year, I suddenly realized that I wasn't sneaking around and finding hidden places to smoke; I was actually advancing in ranks. By this time I had finally realized that I could be a black belt. It was possible. All I needed to do was to show up, practice and practice harder than anyone there. In retrospect, I remember loving the practices, the bruises, the aches and pains. It was the process of putting on the uniform, tying my belt around me, the sparring sessions, the soreness. It was the feeling of ascension to the next level of belief. I began to fall in love with martial arts.

Countless times I would visualize myself wearing my black belt. Little by little, I began to visualize this at home, when I was walking to school, in the garage while sweeping the floors. By the end of my senior year in high school, I finally had the chance to test for that trophy. By this time I had already observed five different black belt tests, and I had literally memorized what the test consisted of. I then began to train as hard as I could in preparation for what I had seen. My sensei, however, had something else in mind for that kid who showed up seven days a week for three or four hours a day. Was what I experienced a geometric progression? It was a seemingly small action done right that over time added up, revealing the geometric potential of success, too large, too fast, and too loud to ignore. It was all about visualizing that one thing I wanted, and emotionally being in the moment. In this case the visualization had to be real in my head, and in order for it to be real, I had to feel it inside my head. I had to see each punch and each kick. I had to visualize what it felt like wearing that black belt every day; if not every time I had a free moment to myself.

Marsha Sinetar, in her book *Developing a 21st Century Mind*, explains two phases. The phases are explained in terms of prompts, used to gather the "kernels of truth amid a field of confusion." Here is a list of things that you can use according to Marsha Sinetar[1]:

Photographs
Poetry
Music
Conversations
Visualization Exercises

In phase two she recommends finding fictional or real-life role models, writing out what you observe from these role models, and examining the feelings and mood—ultimately creating a "written composite of solutions (e.g., with short, vivid paragraphs), we can describe the working world we hope to enter."

---

1   Marsha Sinetar. *Developing a 21st Century Mind*. p. 110-113.

CHAPTER 2

Believe It to Be Possible

THE DAY FINALLY arrived when my sensei gave me the invitation to test for my black belt. Testing day arrived, when I came up to my first sparring opponent. Unbeknownst to me, however, the test was not at all like what I had seen. Every time I fell to the ground gasping for air, I thought, *I was supposed to spar the red belts, not all the black belts*. It was around the third cycle that I finally gave up the thought in my head, and I began to recite like a mantra, "I can do this, get up, get up, breathe, breathe." Toward the end of the sparring session, I was already too tired to worry about the testing changes. Instead, I was focusing on staying present. Why? Because when you are tired, winded, and you are at an end, it requires an enormous amount of concentration just to stay standing and breathing. No different than when you go through a divorce, are financially broke, or beaten by rejection after rejection. You have to stay in the moment and know that every action and step you take will lead to your desired outcome.

Toward the end of my black belt test, I remember falling to my knees. All I could think of was *I can't breathe, I can't stand up, I'm too tired, I should just lie here*. I had seen people test before, too tired to stand up, and still get their black belt. Sure enough I could also just lie there and accept my limitations. But then like an electrical surge another thought came racing through my head. *Get up. You want this or not?* I got up, but after that it only seemed to get more difficult; the air felt heavier, the kicks that landed on me felt more powerful, and it seemed that my opponents were getting faster. It must have been an eternity before my sensei called the test over.

> *"The present moment is the only thing you can't take from anyone. Since this is all they really own."*

—Marcus Aurelius

What is up with the story? For one, whatever situation you find yourself in, always keep a positive mental attitude. The right mental attitude will help you push through tough times. This enables you to keep control of the reactive mind, to control fear, doubt, and self-imposed limitations, simply because you believe it to be possible. Don't kid yourself, life will take shots at you; situations and people will challenge you and downright kick you so hard your knees will give out. Metaphorically speaking, whether you have lived this already or you're about to experience this in your life, it is about how you choose to respond and whether you choose to stand back up. This choice is entirely up to you. The reflection of my own experience gave me a flashback of Julian Edelman's book *Relentless*[2] in which he gives you a glimpse of what his positive mental attitude is about.

> *"The key to achieving isn't looking*
> *at the ultimate goal. It's believing*
> *and then focusing completely on*
> *the next step in front of you."*

—Julian Edelman

---

2 Julian Edelman, with Tom E. Curran. Relentless (2017).

He retells of the formidable comeback the New England Patriots made in Super Bowl LI. They were down 28-3. Now, if you have never watched football, or don't care to watch, it doesn't really matter. Understanding the deficit in score by the third quarter is enough to understand that the team was in a deep, deep hole; most would simply give up and lose morale. But not them, they were notorious for pulling off comebacks, especially at the end, but how? And where did this mental attitude come from? If it was common, all teams would be this way, but they weren't. In Julian Edelman's words, "Coming out of halftime, the Falcons threw one more shovelful of dirt on us and went up 28-3. Finally, it was time to dig out, and everybody grabbed a shovel." Julian Edelman knew that it takes poise, that it takes everything inside you to maintain composure and mental concentration when you are morally, spiritually, and physically exhausted. He knew that it takes one play at a time; that you must stay in the moment. Here is the gold nugget: *Grab a shovel, and start digging yourself out of your hole. No one will shovel for you.* These defining moments occur to us all the time. The difference is that we don't carry around a camera crew, and it's not on national television, but the seconds do "tick on the clock" waiting for you to do something, waiting for you to make the next play. So do something about it!

The Best or Nothing

I still remember when I finally came to live with my stepfather; I wanted to be like him. I was about fifteen then. Having my biological father not care two cents for me, I wanted to impress on this man who took me in. I gave my best effort at everything. But…more effort as I found out doesn't equal more results. What it does teach is to react. Many years later I learned that it is not enough to have muscle memory to succeed and achieve what you want. You have to learn to think almost as things are occurring; like playing chess in high speed, think ahead, think options, think probabilities; all while having a fast reacting time. It's complicated and overwhelming at first, but with practice, guided practice, anything is possible. The question is how can you get to that place? Who can teach you? Where are the gurus?

This became clear to me; no one teaches you how to be your best. Only you will know that. Only you know what your best looks like, what it feels like. For that matter, it is like this for everything.

Here is the mind-blowing thing: no one tells you that when you're young! In fact, no one tells you where to start, who to talk to. It's like you're in a sea, with no land in sight, and then someone tells you, "Just keep swimming, and believe in yourself." But what if you're swimming in the wrong direction! And as it turns out, I did swim out in the wrong direction several times, only to have to turn around to retrace my steps and start over. I've met many people in my life, and I have witnessed them giving up on their dreams and goals. Why?

Because they swam out so far out
in the wrong direction that they
found it too exhausting to swim
back to where they started.

Back in high school I had a good friend. Well, he aspired to be an author, a literary legend as he often put it. He wrote poems, stories, and wrote and wrote. You'd often find him carrying loads of papers, with scribbles and notes. He would show you and you'd think he was a mad scientist trying to figure out some obscure law of metaphysics. But he was proud of what he was creating. You could see the passion and the desire. We graduated and we both went our separate ways. When I was about twenty-three, I heard through another acquaintance that he had moved to San Diego and had given up on writing.

Having personal knowledge of these instances, as you probably might know others, begged me to question, What makes people different? What makes them want to succeed? To push on in spite of obstacles, cultural difference, lack of money, resources, and/or support. In part I had some of these restraints. But my ego would comfort me and tell me, "You're right, it isn't fair that some people get the resources, the money, and the advantages. It's not like I'm the only one going through this." I made constant and several attempts to keep myself pumped and ready. But as human as I am, I found it exhausting. I wanted to give up often and at every turn. Why did I keep pushing? Years later, it finally dawned on me: Talent is something you decide on. It's never outside of you, it's nothing you can buy, rent, or borrow; it's not like you discovered it like Columbus "discovered" the Americas. We have it much easier; we don't have to travel hundreds of miles hoping it will be there. It's already in us. It's sort of like…it just clicks. It's that eureka moment when you realize what that talent is.

I had graduated from high school, and as I saw

it, I had two choices. One, I would start working as a gardener like my school counselors told me, or I would apply for colleges. No offense to landscaping—it's lucrative but it wasn't for me. I had barely accumulated a 2.5 GPA. What prominent colleges would accept a 2.5 GPA? Lucky for me I busted ass my last two years, which reflected Advance Placement classes and straight A's and B's. I had an argument to make and a compelling closing one in every letter. As you can imagine, I was turned down by several colleges, but I was accepted to a small university with small teacher-to-student ratios, great campus life, and amazing Southern California weather. But it was a private school and expensive as hell. Whether I belonged or not, I told myself that I wouldn't care; I wasn't alive to merely exist. Perhaps that was my motivation, or perhaps I knew where I had been, and I knew what going down that road looked like. I didn't want to live in poverty. I didn't want to waste my life in the streets. I wanted to find myself. I wanted to find my passion, and be a person of value. Perhaps knowing what you don't want brings you closer to finding out what you do want. All I knew was that I came with nothing, so it seemed to me at that point, everything was a win.

The Reactive Mind vs.
the Thinking Mind

So far my life had been that of a reactive mind. I'd mimic what others did, thinking that was success. I had learned to react through constant practice. But what of the thinking mind, the critical mind that serves as checks and balances to the reactive mind? Remember about playing chess at high speeds? Well, I had learned to play chess, but speeding up the process and thinking organically was another lesson. Thinking fast, being proactive and with intelligent improvisation was the goal. I had my first experience while practicing martial arts. There, you have to have clarity of mind, you have to think on the fly, think strategy, think ahead, and yet, so fast that you have to let your mind go; you have to let your mind do what it does best, think and react at the same time. Why is this important? Because it rules you when you face your fears, when you are in a situation where your subconscious kicks in. In the field of law enforcement, it is often referred to as "flight, fight, or freeze." Many have experienced it when standing in front of large crowds, when giving a public speech, when interviewing for a job, even when talking to that pretty girl you've been planning on asking out on a date. In other words, you freeze or you manage to get through your self-defeating mechanism. For sake of simplicity, that mechanism is the set of habits that run that script in your head: "I can't, I'm not good enough, and I'll never… I wish but…" We all know them. But what we don't know is that it is merely a script that your mind runs over and over again. Why we have them beats me. The important part is that you can reprogram yourself. Through schooling and the academic world, I found that the academic world attempts to tell us where these self-limiting mechanisms originate and what we can do about them. The problem is, it takes time, lots of time, and I didn't have the luxury of time. Don't fool yourself into believing that you have tomorrow to accomplish what you want today. Now let me be perfectly clear: every day that you do something that inches you closer to what you want, you are in fact taking action and not waiting. The more you wait, the more momentum you create to wait more, so don't wait!

I had to find a way to put myself in a place where I could practice how to "will" myself to move in moments where I freeze. In other words, I had to consciously be aware of my reactive mind, and then begin to use my thinking mind. My closest experience on how to do this was reflected in my martial arts training. This was the beginning of training my mind to overcome what has been used to reacting. I took this experience and I went out on interviews for jobs that my self-imposed complexities (my personal emotional pets) told me I couldn't interview for. I began to weight lift, another thing my self-defeating mechanism told me I didn't have the genes for. I continued to interview and do things out of my comfort zone for several months, until I landed a job with law enforcement. Every training and scenario that the agency puts you through is nerve-wracking. Why wouldn't it be? I was now supposed to save lives, help when no one can, show empathy when no one is around, muscle through fear when all are merely standing by. This was the perfect place where I could practice gaining control of my reactive mind.

Here is the gold nugget: Find a place, a situation, or train yourself to control your fears so that you learn to get out of the "flight, fight, or freeze" syndrome. We are naturally afraid of certain things, and our nervous system will alert us and prompt us to fight, run away, or freeze. But it doesn't have to be this way.

My dad used to tell me, "Giovannelli, if you're not here, where are you? You need to be in the here and now so that you can absorb life around you." What he was really trying to tell me is that if my mind is not really "here," then the mind cannot be available to do what you are asking it to do. My dad was asking me to practice conscious, moment-by-moment awareness. What I didn't know was that by staying in the moment, you don't allow your mind to worry about things that have not happened, and you don't worry about the things that have already happened. In other words, you don't allow your mind to be available to anxiety, depression, regret, anger, fear, the "what if's, the "I should have done this, that," or whatever.

I had come to this country with nothing. I have gone hungry, slept in the streets, been penniless, been married (three times) and divorced (twice), and been told I wasn't capable of going to college. Somehow you either roll over and accept it or you get hungry. I had opted to go out and see what I could do before I died. So, what's the gold nugget here? If you're not hungry yet, get hungry. Those who are persistent usually outperform those with natural-born abilities. It is debilitating when you get stuck on "What if it happens again, what if I can't this time, what if?" Practice conscious moment-by-moment awareness. Here is the thing. We know what we know. Meaning we know what will happen or could happen. We also know what we don't know, meaning the things that we know are out there, but we have no idea how to get to them. And then there are the things that we don't know that we don't know; this is where all possibilities occur, where the magic is! This is when people say, "You miss 100% of the shots you don't take." You simply don't know what possibilities are there for you because you simply haven't tried or won't try.

Remember, conscious moment-by-moment awareness. Then, the real stuff comes along when you begin to operate at an unconscious level with moment-by-moment awareness; meaning you've trained your mind to be in a position to absorb what is happening around you without exerting effort. This conscious moment-by-moment awareness will require energy, it will mentally exhaust you, and quite frankly, you will want to give up practicing. But think of the person you will become once you've trained your mind to be aware! Examine the day-to-day routines of highly successful people; they operate efficiently not because they were born that way, but because they've practiced this moment-by-moment awareness. They no longer exert an enormous amount of energy just trying to figure out what they are going to do with their day. So when do you know you've achieved this awareness? Better yet, how do you know when you've reached that level of mastery or practiced enough to begin to unlock your potential?

Author Grant Cardone offered a solution in his book *The 10X Rule* (2011): Do things ten times more, with ten times more effort, with the right mind-set and the right action. In fact research has found that it takes accumulative efforts, and that it is an estimated 10,000 hours, or an accumulative ten years of practice that elite performers are logging in to help them reach a mastery level. What are *you* accumulating? Here is the research. Elite violinists accumulated 10,000 hours of practice by age twenty. In all, the average completed it in about ten years. I am not sure that these statistics can apply in all disciplines, but as Grant Cardone explains, "It is better to be pleasantly surprised than greatly disappointed." So even if you overshoot your mark, you'll be ahead of what you originally perceived to be possible. Don't be afraid to be obsessed. This is reality of the 10X rule, the reality of how dedication and consistency work. We can call it whatever we want, but in the end, it is about falling in love with what you do.

Of Being a Husband x2...soon to be x3

I wasn't trying to follow Mr. Cardone's formula of 10x with my divorces, if you are wondering. But as it happened, I ended up getting in a rut with this; more troubling were the number of relationships I went through. It isn't usually a good thing when you mention to a girl you've been married and have children. Of course not, you come with not only baggage, but emotional baggage at that. If you're lucky, your divorces are clean cuts. But as in most cases, they never are. The most damaging was my last divorce. That divorce made me realize that I had to make a few changes, but again, each change was not without trials and errors. That change started with my latest marriage. I was more truthful with this new girl than I had ever been and far more blunt about everything. I approached everything with skepticism. For a long time I doubted her every time she would tell me she loved me. All I would hear inside my head was "Yeah right, how many times have you heard that before." But I also heard another me, reminding me that, if I ought to experience something new, then I ought to change some things, starting with my thinking. You wrestle with the voice that tells you to do what's easy and simple. It's easy to listen to that voice, but it always leads to the same path. The path you know you don't want, the path you most likely have already been through. So why go there again? You know what's there; what you don't know is where the alternative leads you to. Once again, it's a win-win situation; I have nothing, so why resist what I want. I had to listen to myself. What you want, wants you. Let go and allow your mind to do what it's best at, think and react at the same time. Take what you know, discard what doesn't work, and try what might work. This is how it works in the dojo. Why can't it work here? Your mind is equipped with more experiences, more life lessons. Your mind does this almost instantly. But we place a governor and limitations. It's a speed trap that keeps your car revving, keeping you stuck in second gear. If we are wiser, why do we do this to ourselves? We should be faster and better decision makers. In my situation I was talking about letting go and allowing this new person into my heart, my life.

But this goes for everything in life. Why should I be afraid to try the very thing that I want, that I desire in my life?

How long are you going to wait before you demand the best for yourself?

—Epictetus, 135 AD

I was first introduced to my wife by her father. Her father and I worked for the same agency. We were at training together, and although we both worked for the same department, we were assigned to different bureaus. Throughout our training I participated, spoke up. I mention this because he was sitting directly behind me, assessing me, evaluating me, and thinking… At the end of the training session, he approached me and started out talking about our department problems, solutions, opportunities, and it just seemed like any other chitchat. Every now and then he'd ask if I had a family, what my educational background was, if I had kids, if I was married. At the time he was a sergeant rank and had been with the bureau for a number of years, just about retirement age. Of course he was skilled at asking the right questions, and when to ask them. He asked me to meet his daughter, "just so that she can have a different perspective." I didn't have a reason to say no. I mean, at the time he outranked me and it was an excellent opportunity to make him my mentor. I got in my car, having already giving him my number. I thought for a moment and asked myself, was I interviewed and I didn't even see it coming? Indeed I was… I was interviewed, and this can happen at any time in our lives. Most often we are surveyed by employers, bosses, prospects, but we are usually not surveyed as a prospect for someone's daughter.

Well, we met and as it turns out, I got married to her. This would mark my third marriage. This time, equipped with conviction to be better, listen more, and love without reservations, I set out to begin a new journey. The first time my son met her he said, "Daddy, can we keep her?" We did keep her, and on December 23, 2016, she gave birth to my second child, Charlotte. We had some bumps along the roads, misunderstandings, miscommunication, and arguments about who was right and who was wrong. In the end, I had to be wiser. I knew what reactions I had made and what actions I had taken in my prior marriages. I knew them well because they operated out of my own "pet" complexities, my self-pity, my self-righteousness; they operated out of my inse-curities, my anger, and my fears. I couldn't react this way anymore, not if I wanted this to be my last and only marriage.

Marriage is work, and more often than not, I had to put aside my need to be right. I had to ask myself, "What outcome are you looking for? Because if you argue and prove her wrong, it doesn't inspire change in her; it will only give her resentment." I had to think in terms of how I was going to lead my family, my children, my wife, my whole life. This new nucleus depends on me and how I react to things. There is no luxury to lash out, to act in a way that is inconsistent with what I want to create. But every day is still work. Taking someone for granted isolates them and prompts them to comply with what you are asking them. Indirectly when you take people or your loved ones for granted, you are giving off the signal that they are not important and to leave you alone. And that is exactly what happens; the universe conspires to give you what you want.

So in everything it is important that you exercise what you want by being present in your speech, in your actions and reactions. The reactions are ruled by your habits and your knee-jerk reactions.

If you want something different, you have to stop that. Control your knee-jerk reactions, study them, and then, change the program. More on this later, but for now begin to pay attention to your reactions and ask yourself, "Is this what I want? Am I happy with the result that I have produced as a result of what I have done?" If the answer is no, then examine this again. Plato once wrote in his recollection of Socrates speeches, "An unexamined life is not worth living." Socrates made this statement to emphasize that we must live fully as humans, to raise our existence above that of mere beast. While Socrates begs humanity to examine itself in a deep philosophical way, what I am asking is for you to examine what you don't like, if you do not like the results you are producing. If you do re-examine your actions, thoughts, and reactions, don't dwell on it as if you have a life sentence. Mistakes, failures, and errors are lessons; they are the best teachers you could have. Treat them as such and let it go.

Oftentimes I tell my wife that I didn't have failed marriages; I was merely prepping and getting better so that when the day came for me to really step up, I would rise to the occasion. Of course she thinks I'm crazy and often laughs when I say this. But if I didn't condition myself to think this way, no one else would do it for me. Eventually I would have been stuck with the thinking that I wasn't made for marriage. In fact, when my co-workers found out that I got married, yet again, one of them said, "Giovannelli, I thought we had this conversation; you are not made for marriage." Of course we never had this conversation, but her statement made me realize that the majority of people are self-defeating by listening to other people's negative influences and opinions, intended or not.

Of Being a Father or a Mentor

Fighting for more than just you is like a rude awakening. It disrupts any self-pity, self-perpetuating, self-destructive mechanism you managed to construct over the course of your life. You want to give up, but when you turn to look down, there is always someone looking up at you. For me it was my son, holding on to my leg, barely a few feet tall. At the time he was just a few years old. He would often look at me as if I was the only person in the universe to protect him. With a task so immense, there is no time to dwell on the unimportant; there's only time to achieve, to protect, to work, and to love better, harder, and more than before. Children tend to tell the truth, so sincere that sometimes it comes off as socially rude. Being a single dad at the time, I realized this when he overheard a conversation I was having on the phone. All he heard is me saying was "I can't, I can't do it anymore." This little boy's response was "Why can't you, Daddy?" as he would continue to casually play, as if he was making a matter-of-fact statement, unbothered by the trivialities of adulthood. I paused for a moment, about to dismiss his statement. But then, it occurred to me, why can't I? It doesn't matter what it is that I think I can't do. It's about being present in the moment and not allowing self-imposed limits to fill my head. Be careful what you utter; words have power.

Why can't I? He is right... The question should really be, why not? Can this little boy be so wise that he is unaware of the lessons he is teaching me? Might he be the very guru that my dad and I have so vivaciously been looking for? By the time he turned three, he reaffirmed a great lesson to me. Just because it seems impossible, it doesn't mean that it is. I remember the moment as if it were yesterday. He was in Tae Kwon Do practicing board breaking. The board was plywood, just about an inch thick. I thought for sure he would hurt himself, cry and bury his head under my arms telling me he couldn't do it. But to my surprise, he conceptualized the break, and broke the board. Now, he didn't break it the first time, or the second time, not even the third time. He had to practice breaking a plastic pre-broken board, and just about an hour of instruction on how to "follow through" with his momentum, the force, and the foot. He had to visualize his foot going through the board. But he was three years old! Isn't this concept too far advanced for his age? So I thought... So how is it that a three-year-old can believe it to be possible? Because no one is telling him that it isn't. He isn't bothered by other people's self-imposed, limiting beliefs; at that age there is barely a self-limiting belief to begin with. But, there he was, in front of about fifteen parents, his classmates, and several instructors. As his instructor yelled, "Begin," this little boy approached, bowed, and jumped into a fighting stance. He then moved in and threw a hook kick, breaking the board! His instructor holding the board was caught off guard. Surprised at what just happened, he looked at the broken board with disbelief! Everyone applauded as this little boy looked around with a confused look, like saying,

"Can't everyone do it too?" It was a sight to see, and luckily I managed to record that moment on my phone. Today, I glance at it as a reminder that anything is possible.

This little boy was proving to be the very mentor my father and I were seeking. It would seem that being a father is both being a mentor and being a student. And simultaneously I had to acknowledge that and be ready to take on both; no matter the source or how inexperienced I thought the source was from. I realized that through my son's casual questioning, he prompted me to analyze through problem-based learning and critical thinking. As the weeks turned into months, and months into years, he was growing wiser and ready to ask more and more questions. Questions that continuously led me to rethink and reexamine what I was caught in the moment with. Isn't this what a mentor is supposed to do; to transfer knowledge, skills, and attitudes in a way that makes the student arrive at the conclusions through critical thinking? As the relationship grows from mentor to student, there is a behavioral shift that directs the student toward "figuring out" self-discovery through progressive learning, or progressive overload, as we will speak later on. In fact, sometimes my son would challenge my thought process and play devil's advocate without even knowing.

A eureka moment appeared. Mentors are all around; we just shut them off because we think they're too young, they're too old, we think we know more than they do, or we pass judgment and say, "I make more money." Our own ego-driven narcissism drives us to blindness. Perhaps it's the romanticism, the illusion of mentors we see in movies that bursts our bubble of ever finding one or meeting one. But as it turns out, they're everywhere. You just have to open your eyes and listen, ask, and be ready to get it through means you might not think or feel possible.

Of Being a Son

It's hard to decide where to start with this. Did I become a son when I was nine years old, back when I met my stepfather, or did it start when I was fifteen, when I finally moved in with him? For those of you who haven't heard about the Chinese bamboo tree, it is said that in the first year there is no visible sign of growth. While the farmer continues to water it and fertilize it, the second, third, and fourth year go on by with no sign of growth. On the fifth year, the bamboo tree finally breaks ground. The question is, did the bamboo tree grow in five years or on the fifth year? Would the bamboo tree stop growing underground had the farmer stopped watering and fertilizing? Or would it have mattered at all?

When I was nine my stepfather had already planted the seeds in my head. I had known him briefly around that age. And for just a few months, he showed up, taught me, gave me attention, and made me feel important. But as brief as it was, it wasn't until I was fifteen that I was challenged with what he had let grow inside my head. Fast-forward many years into the future, and he had passed away. I remember when I heard the news. I was driving a U-Haul truck, moving to a new rental with my newborn and my second wife. By then I was already having too many problems to recount in this section, but to say the least, I was getting ready to leave the relationship. I was driving when I got the call from my mother. "Son, your dad left…" My vision got small, blurry, and my body got numb almost instantly, starting with my hands, then through my torso and feet. I barely managed to pull off the road. I cried and yelled at the same time. It felt like I was drowning, desperately gasping for air to breathe, choked by desperation and tied by anxiety, slowly sinking to the bottom. It must have taken me several minutes that seemed like hours to gather myself again. He was my hero, my guru; and he was gone. I hadn't yet been able to give him my greatest accomplishments; I hadn't yet been able to tell him that I really loved him. I hadn't yet been able to show him that all his lessons, sermons, and faith in me were all for something. I was too late. Was I crying for me?

> *"I am a spiritual being residing in the magnificent human body. I am the universal mind's expression of love, wisdom, beauty, wealth, and charisma. That is who I am, so be it."*

—Alexander Jagiello, 1960-2015
Amtrak Onboard Chief, Coast Starlight

A couple of weeks later I was able to fly out to Washington State from California. I met my mother at the airport. We hugged and cried. I felt her anxiety, her desperation, and her heart beating too fast. I didn't think she knew she was pumping so much adrenaline. She looked like she hadn't slept in days. She was manic, almost not there at all.

We had finally made arrangements for crema-
tion; and together we mourned. We thought we
did, but the reality was that we were in shock.
My dad believed that he was part of the universe,
and that the universe was part of him. Family and
friends gathered to pay respects a day later. I was
asked to say a few words about my dad. It's funny
how we always remember what is told to us repeatedly. Dad would always tell me that I needed
to first visualize and see what I wanted. Then I
needed to decide that it is possible to have and
achieve it. Then decide that it is possible and do
it. He saw the cup half full, and always found the
"why not" from every excuse.

See that it is there.
See that it is possible.
Decide that it is possible and do it!

Be patient with your progress. You will likely not
see any "sprouts" of success right away, but this
doesn't mean it isn't happening. Seeing that it is
possible, visualizing that it is possible and de-
ciding on it is how you water it. As you have
surely noticed by now, even if we allow our habits to run amok, it turns out that our bamboo
tree (results of our habits/success) is not quite

straight. We can still tame it, harder, yes, but not impossible.

What will you do with What Happens to You?

When I departed Washington, I felt like it was all surreal, like it was all a dream. Every night I'd check my voicemails thinking he had left one for me, like he always did. I'd get excited about an idea and I was ready to dial his number. Only to look down at my phone, with my thumb at his speed dial number. He wasn't there anymore. There wasn't anyone at the other end. I remember swallowing hard many times, holding back my tears. I had to keep my composure; I didn't have time to grieve for my dad. I had a bigger problem to contend with. My second wife at the time (my son's mother) was held hostage by a demon that not even the power of love could release her from. The demon took no prisoners and had neither pity nor an ounce of empathy. I'd plead and beg for her strength to break the chains, "Do it for your baby." But…she had already sold her soul; she was in debt to this demon, to addiction, to opiates.

Watching her self-destruct was maddening. I

couldn't do anything about it. Every day she made promises that couldn't be kept. He heart meant every word, but how could she promise when the evil that owned her only cashed out more of her. Days turned into weeks, weeks into months, and before months could turn into years, I had to make a decision.

I pleaded with her parents for help. But as it happens often, the plea fell on deaf ears. Could it be that it was pride that prevented them from seeing the real problem with their daughter? Could she have fooled everyone so well that her lies and deception were that good? Or did they simply want to wash their hands off a problem they could no longer control? Whatever the reason, the outcome was the same. It was up to me to make a decision and make it happen. There are no victims in this story, only those who choose to make themselves one. So, what will you do with what happens to you?

The lesson is simple. You don't have to be a celebrity to experience tragedy or be in a reality show. We all go through our own issues and problems. Some of us will allow what happens to us to dictate our life, but it doesn't have to be this way. We can choose what we do with what happens to us. These series of events were quite difficult for me. I had to pull out every lesson and remember why and how I got every life scar. It was quite an overload that at times I didn't know if I was going get through. Sometimes you won't have time to prepare. The experience alone is the preparation and the test itself.

CHAPTER 3

Accept the reality before you, or change it

WITH MY DAD now deceased, a wife who was addicted to opiates, and a newborn preemie going through opiate withdrawals—still inside a capsule with feeding tubes—it was clear I had problems. With lack of human touch, the only sense of warmth my son had the first month of his life on earth…was a lamp. He was to remain at the Neonatal Intensive Care Unit (NICU) for two more months at least. I had just come back home from a double shift at work one night, a sixteen-hour. I remember walking through the door, and there my son's mother was. She was passed out on the floor with the dog licking her face. The TV was so loud that I had to wonder how long she had been lying there. I had already experienced too many incidents with her, and this was just another one. I checked her pulse and checked if she was breathing; she was and that was a relief. As I shook her, I yelled at her, "What did you take, what did you take?" It took several minutes to wake her up, but even then, she was still disoriented. She didn't smell like alcohol, but had all the symptoms. I confronted her, yet again like many other days. Same excuse, just like many other days. I couldn't take it anymore. I kept thinking, *We have a baby in the hospital*, perhaps more scared than her. *He hasn't felt a human since his existence in the world.* As I began to feel overwhelmed that I could not help my son's mother from herself, I dashed to her purse. I kept yelling at her, "What did you take? You promised me you wouldn't take any more pills." I emptied her purse, and there it was; a prescription pill bottle. I didn't recall ever seeing this bottle.

I examined it, and it read, "Ernest (xxxx)." I distinctly remember her telling me that this Ernest guy was selling pills to clients at the outpatient program that she was attending, and was often trading pills for sex. All sort of things went through my head. I was mad, frustrated, and felt humiliated. My heart was racing out of my chest, and I couldn't slow down. By then, I had already warned her that if she continued to use, it would force me to leave her, and I would have to leave with our son. I didn't say any more. How could I? How can someone say anything to someone who can barely understand or stay coherent? All my thoughts were telling me to stay quiet, to remain composed. And then...my lips moved. I asked her, "Where did you get this?" She said, "I was holding it for a friend." In a callous moment, I chuckled. How was this funny? I still don't know. I calmed myself and I said, "How can you really expect me to believe that? You're thirty years old, leave that to teenagers."

I called the police and reported that my wife was in possession of someone else's prescribed narcotics. They didn't seem to care, to say the least; they didn't even come out to the residence. I needed help, and it seemed that the louder I screamed for it, the quieter it got. I had no choice.

The hardest decisions are not always easy

That night I called my mother. The only living relative I had left. "Mom, I need your help, please. I've never asked you for anything." Of course, just like back when I asked her when I was fifteen years old, what's a mother's love to her only son to say? "I'll be there." That same night I decided I would find an apartment and move out. Easier said than done when you have bills and are tied up to debt. This reality isn't new, and certainly not the last in human history. But the self-limiting questions—Will I make it? Can I do it? Will I survive?—all of those things run through your head like a blazing migraine. I remember shaking my head and telling myself, *Let's just do the math. It will cost $800 for rent, plus the first and last month's rent to get in. That will be $2,400. Plus utility setup, the application fee, and the moving expenses. Plus, the expense to close out any and all accounts tied to my spouse.* As the number started to climb, I asked, *How does a single parent do it? How does anyone? Not to mention I still have to go through the legal process of a divorce!*

Sometimes the numbers will not add up, and things will happen. Because once you desire something with intensity, the universe will begin to conspire to make it happen. You won't know how, when, with whom, or who will facilitate it. This lesson I learned, and it proved to have occurred many times over in my life. So it isn't something that happens as a mere coincidence.

But you have to train yourself to see it, much like training yourself to see opportunities rather than obstacles.

I had to leave, I had no choice. I could no longer torture myself and see the woman I loved inflict harm to herself. I had to teach my son one lesson: you can't fix other people, and just because you can't fix them, it doesn't mean you have to serve their emotional and mental prison sentence with them. Of course through the process, guilt is always the demon that demoralizes you. It's the demon that tells you that you have the obligation to stay, the demon that reminds you of the vows you made in marriage, the sacrifices and the commitment you had made when you professed your love to her. But where was her commitment, her love, and her willpower to overcome what can't be overcome, the willpower to overcome what can't be moved? Love is supposed to fix this! I was infuriated and frustrated. I couldn't stop my migraine, constantly pounding the thoughts. I had to make a decision, I had to leave.

In your trials, you will be challenged and you will be scared. Scared of the "what if's." You will know deep inside that you will have to take action. No one has to tell you this; it is like an innate feeling, but somehow it's the belief that things will change, or the fear that you will never be okay again. Well, you are right on both. Things will never be the same, and you will be okay. You'll have to grab your shovel and start digging your way out. This will mean that you will have to fight through your fear; you'll even have to ignore what people tell you and their opinions. Yes, things sometimes don't seem fair.

The universe conspires to give you what you want; you just have to ask for it

That afternoon, I made phone calls, asked for quotes, and started packing. I was not going to lose my son at the expense of my wife's addiction. He didn't deserve this, and at the very least, he would have a father. I was armed with more motivation, a deep desire to succeed. I had no choice. But... Still... *How will I do this?* I was mad at myself. Why did I wait so long? Was it that I hoped my wife would miraculously get better? I made a promise to myself that day that I would not wait for a catastrophe to occur for me to take action. I've seen people immobilized by fear, doubt, and contentment for the mediocre. I could no longer afford the luxury of time. I had to teach my son to be strong and resilient.

Two biggest battles awaited me, however: the actual process of the divorce, and having to explain to my son later in life why his mother cashed out her hopes for Xanax, Vicodin, and Percocet. I had no clue how I was going to explain this, while making him understand that he has the right to live, without her if necessary. I was still mad at my birth father for abandoning me. How was I supposed to teach my son a concept I had yet to understand?

Of Broken Pride

Shortly thereafter, my son's mother was arrested for falsifying prescriptions. As you would imagine, she was placed under investigation at work for her arrest. Every time I walked in the job, it felt humiliating. My colleagues, her peers, our management knew. How do you walk into work and keep from breaking? Everywhere you turn there is suspicion that you had something to do with it, that you somehow caused it, or you're involved. That's the general consensus at least, and you feel it the moment you walk inside. The people who spoke to you now don't; the people who laughed with you now meet you with a cold shoulder and whispers. You're an island. Once again, I was faced with critical decisions to make. I didn't have the luxury of caring what they thought of me. I didn't have the luxury of time, and I didn't have time to grieve for my wife's despair and addiction. I had lost her, just like I had lost my father. I had to push forward.

Day after day, you somehow just have to push yourself. But you're reminded minute by minute of what you don't have, of what you had, of what you lost. The day came when my work called me to interview me about my wife's crimes. "Did you know?" My voice shook a bit, my throat closed, and it got harder to take a deep breath. "I'll remind you of the Code of Silence." How could I have known? I blamed myself for a long time; I was supposed to be an expert at spotting lies… deception. I was a field probation officer. I had supervised juveniles and adults, and I had managed drug programs. But somehow I missed it. The truth was painful when I realized how far along she was with her addiction. I could not save her. No one could have saved her. I was vulnerable, humiliated, and exhausted. Some part of me wished no one knew, but as it turned out, everyone knew. When it was finally over I walked off the interview feeling…hurt. I had to tell the tribune of the pain I had to endure, of how I was lied to, of how I was deceived.

No matter how much my pride hurt, I already knew what it was to come with nothing, to have nothing. I had slept on benches before; I had gone hungry for days in my past, and on my best days I would count pennies to buy a sixty-nine-cent burrito. Somehow I knew I would be able to get past this. I think what hurt the most was that I thought I had finally been done with pain. I thought that I was finally pardoned by GOD and given the opportunity of love and happiness. Instead, it was yet another lesson; it was more pounding under more pressure; life was pushing me just over my coping capacity, just enough to progressively overload what I could handle.

My son's grandfather, seeing what was going on, stepped in—not to help me, but to assume rights over my son. I know now that he, too, was a victim of his daughter's lies. We were pitted against each other in a gladiator fight inside the courtroom over custody of my son. It was not brawn that mattered here; it was wit, intelligence, and money that armed you with a likely win scenario. In a series of court sessions, at first we were all just representing ourselves. It was a battle for my son's custody. They won one, I would win others. It wasn't until about the fourth court session that my son's grandfather somehow acquired temporary custody rights. How did this happen? I had stable employment and did not have any history of addiction. How did this happen? He outwitted me with bureaucratic accuracy, mountains of forms, and un-dissectible mazes of paper, deadlines, and court fees. Court session was over, and I walked over to him. I cried in a plea, "This isn't a criminal proceeding of yours; it's your grandson. You know it's wrong, and you know your daughter can't care for him, so why would you do this?" He looked down at me and said, "The judge made his decision."

As I walked away, I knew it wasn't going to be easy, and it wasn't going to end pretty. This fight was to the end. I could not spare anyone's feelings, least of all my own. I had to grow emotional calluses fast. I did more research, and behold, I found her. An attorney as tough as the one they had. The court battle went on for another year, exchanging accusations after accusations. I was the bad guy of course, I was the one asking for the divorce, I was the one with the good job, and I was the one leaving the alleged poor woman who had nothing. Somehow, however, my son's grandfather managed to evade his daughter's addiction in court, time and time again. He was cunning. How could he not be? He had been an attorney for the county for well over twenty years, and we were fighting in his turf.

But...as life had taught me, things don't always have to add up. You have to be truthful with yourself, and your desire has to be so intense that there is nothing else in this universe. I had faith, and if I lost, at least my son would know I had lost at the Coliseum, having fought for a cause bigger than I was. I was determined to fight even if it meant homelessness and being penniless.

Here it is again, the gold nugget. You have to be willing to go all the way in pursuit of your dreams and goals. You can't just wish for something and be halfway committed. It won't work. Your mind immediately begins to work in a way that you will see alternatives and opportunities you weren't able to see previously. When you are fully committed, you leave your mind no choice but to look for answers. Just as Hernan Cortes in

1519 did when he burned his ships, sending a clear message to his men: you either win or you perish; there is no turning back.

And indeed, in a way, that is exactly what it took. I had to "rob Peter to pay Paul" every month. I had to work double shifts every day to make ends meet, to pay for my attorney, for court fees, child support, spousal support, food, rent—all for a marriage that lasted little over two years. I didn't have time to grieve for my dad, didn't have time to spare anyone and least of all my emotions.

Days turned into weeks, weeks into months, and months into years. I was exhausted. But I couldn't quit. I needed the money to get my son back. He needs to know that I fought for him, that he has a father; his birth father (unlike the one I had) stood by him through hell's purgatory. He needs to know that his father stood for a cause, and just like Atlas was condemned to carry the sky on his shoulders for having opposed the Olympians, I, too, would gladly hold the sky for my son so he may see that no Olympian GOD in that court could break his father's pride and love for his son. I knew that one day my son's grandfather would also have to face the truth about his daughter.

Allow me to rephrase this. Don't go in halfway. You have to go in all the way, commit. I won't lie to you, to commit also means that things can fall apart. Don't kid yourself into believing that nothing will happen. But also know that when you commit, your mind begins to work in a way that solves problems efficiently. People around you will be inspired and will join you, help you, support you. This is the side effect of committing. There were in fact people at work who cheered me on. And while their cheer was afar, witnessing their muffled cries for me to push on through the sidelines always pushed me beyond what I thought to be possible. Remember this, everything counts, everyone, even your local barista who serves you coffee every morning remembers your name and how you like your favorite latte.

Breakthrough

Toward the end of the custody battle, my son's mother and I were doing a visit exchange with my son. She grabbed onto my arm and bruised me. She had been mad that the spousal support wasn't enough. I took this to court and asked for a trial. My attorney thought I was crazy and advised me to stop calling Child Protective Services.

I told her, "Believe me, every time I exchange my son with her for visits, she is high. She's placing a child in danger!"

With a long sigh, she looked at me and said, "What about this injury you claim she gave you?"

I said, "Well, she did, and she is high right now."

She paused for a minute, turned to look at her and then looked back at me, and said, "Okay." The judge then asked both attorneys to chambers. About twenty minutes later, they all came out. My attorney said, "Look, if you are wrong in this, you will lose everything. Right now the court sees you as an overbearing father, overreacting, with no factual basis. But if you are willing to waive the trial and drop the allegations of assault from your wife, the judge will order a drug test today."

My heart was pounding hard, I could hardly hear anyone else, my legs and my arms were feeling numb, my hands were shaking, and my stomach was spasming with nervous contractions. I said, "Yes, let's do this." I knew that a failure to test would be considered a positive test, but I was hoping she showed up. I wanted not only closure that affirmed she was using, but also proof that I was doing right in protecting my son.

A few days later I received a call from my attorney's office. The secretary asked me, "Where are you? Are you where I can speak to you?"

"I can speak now; do you have any information about the drug test?"

"I do, but if you're driving, you need to pull over. She tested positive, but there's more. The lab said they don't know how she is still alive. She's a ticking time bomb. She has so much in her system that she should have overdosed long ago."

"What!?" I exclaimed as my tears rolled out and my voice shook with anger and sadness. "What now, when can I get my son?"

"The judge has signed to turn your son over forthwith, with full physical and legal custody, to you. You can pick up the paperwork from our office and go pick up your son today."

When I arrived at the office to pick up the paperwork, I was shown the numbers, the data, and the results of the drug test. The therapeutic levels were 500 mg; she tested at 76,000 mg of meth-amphetamine. I was shocked and relieved. As for my son's grandfather, I'm sure he, too, suffered humiliation and emotional stress. After all, it was his daughter, not just a client at work who lost the case in court. I had to forgive for my son's sake. I had to teach my son to forgive and to let go of any pet complexities we think we have.

Why this long, drawn-out story? We all face our trials and tribulations. They come in all shapes and sizes. Some more complex and more painful than others. But in the end, we all have to face the same lessons. We all have to push through and see it through. It's in these moments that you have to pull yourself together, and draw from all your experiences. If you haven't mentally prepared to take on these types of emotional and spiritu-al loads, you will find it hard, even debilitating. Begin to train your mind, or loads that exceed your capacity to take action will crush you. Know and understand what anchors you, what grounds you. You need to know what you fight for, what you are passionate about.

CHAPTER 4

Forging an Unstoppable Attitude

I WAS PAYING for my attritions, but was I? Or was I being forged, made... Perhaps I was meant to be broken before I could be given more? Being the martial arts aficionado that I was, of course I had come across Bruce Lee's wisdom. To paraphrase one of many things this man had said, if you fill your cup with water, it can no longer take any more; it's too full. If you wish to learn, you must empty the cup.

I had asked many people—professors, friends, colleagues—what they thought about this; they all agree that at some point you must empty the cup. But what about those who refuse to let go of the water they currently hold in the cup? The water being all the accumulated information, the preconceived notions of life, and how things "should be" according to how we were raised.

One of my later best friends had interpersonal issues with relationships. He felt the need "to belong." In his own right he was extremely successful and hardworking. At one point he was worth 1.2 million in real estate, mainly through owning various properties and rentals. But there was always something missing in his life. Later I came to find that as he was growing up, he had been through the system in foster care, adoption agencies, and bounced from home to home. In spite of that he managed to focus his efforts in school and make success. But there was always his fear and anxiety of being alone. By all accounts, he was. With no family and a few friends he managed to make along his life, he had a few people he could count on. I could see his victimization, his recording loop playing over and over again. But at what point are you willing to stop that recording? Or can you even stop it?

I asked myself, *How did I do it?* I sat on it for a while until it came to me. It was my attitude toward how I saw things; perhaps it was my perspective, but it was always my attitude at the end of the day. I had come to terms with the fact that

I would live without people in my life, so it was never again a concern or at the top of my priority list. Now don't get me wrong, we all wish to belong and even create our very own family. But it isn't so much of a preoccupation that it literally incapacitates your daily routines. It was for my best friend, and it hurt me to see him this way. Relationship after relationship he would not let go of them no matter how destructive they would be. There was always an excuse why his situation was somehow different.

Reprogramming the Operating System

So I went to work on this question. How does one let go and forge an unstoppable attitude? I came across several readings, motivational speakers, and seminars. I was curious how this worked. I knew that if I somehow found or shed a bit of light into this, I would not only help my buddy, but begin to formulate a cautionary manual for myself. Like a failsafe switch if I ever found myself holding on to someone or something that was destructive to my well-being. I began to go through my journals to see where the points of change occurred in my life, and what I did. I then began to read authors and books where change was imminent.

Who I was, was nothing more than a series of habits that I had learned over time. These "things" we learn are acquired by social norms, family taboos, the academic world that tells you what should be, not be; it is the hurt, the pain, the love. It is basically everything we learn to do or avoid. So naturally our brain begins to form a series of algorithms that evoke "go, stop, caution, run, fear, feel good." If we begin to work on the habits (our program), we can essentially create a different algorithm for success, attachment, love, friendship, etc. Could this be possible? I was excited to feel that this may be true. I was excited to realize that if I could work on a set of concrete ideas and methods, perhaps I would have a chance of letting go of everything and begin to design my life as I wished it.

I went forth looking at religion, new age methods, meditation, and the spiritual. The more I looked, the more my dad became present in my life again. He was gone, but he was more part of me now than ever before. Perhaps this was what he was looking for, a way to uncover his blindfolds, a way to see the world as it truly is. While meditating on this, I began to remember that my dad never really told Mom and me of his misery, of his struggles, or his childhood. When I asked him why, he'd say, "For what? What's done is done, and now I'm living my happiest with you guys. Listen, Giovannelli, you have to live in the present. The past is gone, and the future isn't here yet. So where are you now?"

I'd answer, "I'm here, Dad."

And he'd say, "Then be here, and stay here. Breathe, look, and let go of what doesn't matter."

"But, Dad, how do you know what doesn't matter?"

"You don't; what matters now may not matter later and vice versa."

At the time some of it made sense, but other things did not. Now with this recollection, I can say that every defining moment in my life changes had something to do with letting go and being in the present. Let me examine this again:

1. On the things to do; just do it. Decide that it is possible and do it.
2. Your attitude makes or breaks you.
3. Live in the present (what's done is done,

the future isn't here, so where are you?).
4. See that it is possible.

Armed with these basic tenets, I realized that part of letting go of things and seeing that things are possible has to do with knowing that we are an accumulation of habits. If habits can be reprogrammed, then we can create new habits, hence a new algorithm.

So I called my buddy and explained to him that we are habits. I asked him, "If you could change a habit of feeling helpless, would you?" He answered that he would. Knowing that he was an IT guy, I asked him, "What happens if the operating system in a computer fails to load? You know that the computer has great potential, great hardware, but the operating system always fails to load. Would you continue to use it in hopes that maybe one day it will load?"

I didn't hear a sound out of him. Finally after several seconds of silence, he responded, "I'd toss the computer and get a new one."

So I asked him, "Why aren't you the programmer of your life. It's like doing the same thing over and over again expecting different results.

Isn't that the definition of insanity? Buddy, you're stuck in a loop, a loop you created." I then asked him, "You're a programmer. Tell me how a loop works."

"Okay, so if you want to program a computer to perform a task that repeats like a specific operation multiple times, you make controlled statements. This would be the body of a loop. The body of a loop gets executed repeatedly until the condition becomes false or the programmer breaks the loop." My buddy stopped in what sounded like mid-sentence.

I then said, "There you go. You are the only one who has the power to break the loop. You're running on an automatic mode that you're not even aware of."

"If you want something you never had,
you have to do things you've never done."

—Unknown

This quote finally made sense. What was interesting about the conversation I had with my buddy was that you have to speak in the language that people understand best. If I tell a religious person to change their program, he'd be as confused as my buddy would be if I'd asked him to have faith. It has to make sense to them, in the language that they speak the most, most of the time. My buddy is religious, but he can only make sense of life if it has logic and algorithms. Could this be why so many people can't break their loops? Perhaps it isn't so much that they aren't capable of change as much as it is not having the right tools or the right language. It suddenly made so much sense to me. I'm sure I have not been the only one to know this. I knew then that it wasn't about reinventing the wheel; it was about sharing my stories and reinventing myself. This was exciting.

As for my buddy, he is still meditating on this. Will I ever give up on him? No. It will make sense to him eventually. If it never does, then the journey of self-reinvention was inched forward with his help. For that I will be eternally grateful to him.

Are you worth it?

This begged more inquiry into the matter. Most people, it seems, know what they have to do, yet they are paralyzed to move into action. Why? Like my buddy, who knows that his relationship is destructive, yet he continues to be paralyzed.

As I mentioned earlier, while I was going through my second divorce, I was plagued with anxiety. In an effort to address my "malfunction," I went to see a therapist. As you might have guessed, he referred me to an anxiety group. Our group met weekly and together we were educated on the matter. One thing about group therapy, all members in attendance feel the need and the entitlement to chime into your problem and give you advice. It works for some, and in other cases it can be a very powerful tool as people end up realizing that they are not alone in their struggles. However, in yet other instances you end up watching how people feel worthless and helpless. They just can't seem to find their own voice, their worth. You can hear it when they speak. Every meaning behind their words is minimized; everything is spoken as small and insignificant. You've heard it too with people at work or at the coffee shop: "I have a small business idea; it's not that big of an achievement" or "I don't really look that great. I will never get the promotion" or "I only got the promotion because no one else applied." It's the very language they use every day that is minuscule, minimizes their achievements, their triumphs, and their passions. My dad came to mind yet again. Over and over again he'd preach to me, "Giovanelli, use your words wisely; they determine what and who you are. The Universe hears you and gives you what you want. And it all starts with what you say." My mother can attest to this, as she would watch me in frustration. Now I can see, he wasn't too far off; he was on to something.

So what do your words tell you? Are you small? Worth change, worth a promotion? Do you speak of yourself with self-respect? So why can't my buddy see this? Does he, in spite of all the knowledge he possesses, feel worthless? It is obvious he has created his own reality, and he hangs on to it because he knows it. He fears the unknown more, and that paralyzes him from any possible change. He'd rather keep doing what he's always done, because although cruel and miserable, he believes it is safer than the alternative; the possibility of being alone, forever.

This was a powerful concept. I had already known this; in fact I had studied it at the University of Redlands, in my undergraduate studies in sociology. So what was new this time? It pertained to my closest friend, and if I wasn't careful, it could pertain to me as well. When the information is outside of you, you frankly don't care; but everything changes when you are in the middle of it.

What now? What can I do to make sure that it doesn't happen? Or at least so that I can see it as it occurs. I sat on the thought, and I left it. I went about my days at work, until one day I was sitting at the table with my third wife, talking about how well adjusted our children were. The more we spoke about it, the more we both came to the realization that it was because we held ourselves and our children accountable for every detail that derails us in the wrong direction; hence an immediate feedback and rewards system. Could something this simple be the answer?

So, here it is:

1. Hold yourself accountable for every detail that derails you from your goal.
2. Force yourself for immediate feedback and reward yourself for the things well done.
3. Accept where you are, and the responsibility of where you want to go.

These three rudimentary concepts seemed easy enough to digest; and in retrospect, they all were evident in my case, as you will see here.

I had taken my son to the movies; somewhere toward the end he began to cry and scream that he wanted to leave. It was obvious he was scared at the scene in the movie. I hurdled out in a hurry, pushing my son out of the movie theater. He continued to cry while he followed behind me, desperately asking me not to be mad at him. I didn't want to answer him, because I felt that if I did I would lash out at him. This was no reason to be mad at a child. What was it? Why was I so angry? When we finally got to the car, he caught up to me and said, "I'm ready to talk, Daddy. I'm not crying anymore. I got scared, Daddy."

Still furious, I answered in the calmest voice I could muster. "Son, nothing can hurt you, nothing can make you scared, only what you allow. You have to learn to control your emotions." When I asked him to repeat what he understood, he repeated, "I have to control my emotions." I knew he only got half the lesson. We drove back home. In that hour or so to get back home, I decided to treat him to an ice cream. We sat at the bench, caressed by a cool and windy mountain breeze. It was then that I was able to speak to him. "Son, I'm sorry for getting angry at you. I was angry because you were scared. It's okay to be scared.

You're brave and I am very proud of you." By then he was happy again, singing and whistling happy tunes. I wish I could forgive as easily as he did. It hit me then. I wasn't angry at him. At the moment when he was scared and wanted to leave, I perceived weakness. I saw myself as a child, scared, and no one around to help me, encourage me, or believe in me. I hadn't asked to be born, I hadn't asked... Why did my biological father bring me here if he wanted me so bad, only to give me his back? I remember wanting his warmth, his companionship, his presence. But as I waited each and every day, he never came. I had almost forgotten his face, until I was twelve years old. My mother told me I had to live with him. I was excited, but to my dismay, nothing ever came of it when I finally arrived at his doorstep. I was angry at my son, not because of the natural response of a child being scared, but because it felt unfair that I had to face fear alone. I felt like yelling at my son and telling him to suck it up. But that was not on him. That was my "stuff" that came out. It was me, not him, who I saw scared and crying.

I had accumulated so much anger over the years at my birth father. He had another son, yet as I grew older I kept asking, why him and not me? I was more successful, fit, I had a better job, and I was much better-looking. But still, I could not win my birth father's attention and affection over his other son. It was then that I realized my anger had only been repressed. Ignored by the speed of life, money, promotions at work, girlfriends, marriage, divorce, my son, court, struggles, my ego; until now, that is. I urged myself to forgive. Yet, that day I could not. I hated the man; I despised him. "I am not like him," I had to tell myself many times over. I had to teach my son better, but how could I drop this insatiable anger when all I could remember was him choosing another, tossing me aside like I was worthless? I have no other memory. It's like my mind blocked everything out. Then my memories jumped straight to when I was nine years old. So what happened to my memories when I was younger than nine? I did have one memory. I thought that the memory of a beating was all a nightmare, but it was reaffirmed to me when an MRI revealed an old fracture in my tailbone. The doctor said, "It must be from a hard fall. It's old, so most likely from childhood." Funny, I don't remember ever falling so hard that it would cause a fracture in my tailbone. My mother had told me a story once. She said she walked into the house and saw me with a black eye, beaten and quiet in a corner. She had asked her husband (my birth father) what happened. I eagerly awaited his answer, but not even my mother had an answer. That's because he had none. Now I know what it was: his inadequacies and fear led him to beat me. I'm not excusing him by any means. Instead, my anger grew and kept growing over the years.

I cannot wait to forgive; I cannot wait until "something" happens. I can't wait until a catastrophe is upon me to grow. I have to figure it out now. In a moment of reflection, I was glad I asked my son to forgive me for getting upset, and affirming that I was proud of him. I managed to do that in time, without later regretting being too late. But I am still angry and wanting to inflict pain and fear into my birth father's eyes. This is certainly not what my dad would want me to do.

It is clear to me that it doesn't matter what the story is. If I had my birth father, yet witnessed more abuse, in the end, it would have been the same repressed anger. For some people it is their mothers who neglected them, the addiction, the sister, the brother, the sexual abuse, the neglect, the orphanage, or the foster homes. The story varies, but the feelings are the same, the anger and anxiety, the mania, the sleepless paranoia.

It's hard to let go, mainly because I had perceived that the anger was part of who I was, and what I had become. It was part of my success, my triumphs, and my failures. To let go of my anger is to let go of what and who I am. If I let go, then who am I?

I am not claiming to be a guru. But where to find them? When you Google self-help gurus, seminars and popular "personalities" pop up. Some may be legitimate, while others are simply charlatans. So in the meantime, what does one do? I did go to therapy. When you're trying to dig yourself out, even a spoon is a blessing.

In therapy I learned about Ellen Bowers, PhD, author of *The Everything Guide to Cognitive Behavioral Therapy* (2013). She explains how this therapeutic model can help us gain control of our mind. Cognitive behavior therapy states that it can teach to distinguish between thoughts and emotions, and help the person understand automatic thoughts. We can certainly reach a progressive realization of awareness by other means. According to the therapeutic model, many destructive behaviors like addictions, anxiety, post-traumatic stress disorders, and the like are maladaptive behaviors. So where do these maladaptive behaviors come from? Psychologists term these unwanted negative thoughts as irrational thoughts or automatic thinking—rooted in knee-jerk reactions and responses. Hence, as a result of unsupervised, unmonitored thoughts and feelings. By no means is this model perfect, as it only deals with the intellectual capacity of the person to realize their problem. It leaves out other aspects as you will continue to discover as you read on. However, sometimes finding a guru can be difficult. You can start with including this in your tool box until you find one.

Remember, whatever your mind brings itself to believe, it will achieve. The issue here is that too many of us allow our thoughts and our feelings to run amok, with no supervision, training, or structure in which it can flourish.

How to get the fight back in you

On my son's last week of class, I attended a family school outing to the lake. My son was so excited to get in the water that he didn't wait for me. I saw him from a distance as he put on a life jacket. I worried for a minute or two, until I realized that the water was no deeper than about mid-thigh. My son quickly got on the kayak and together with a little girl, they went off. By the time I took out my phone to take pictures, he was already in the middle of the lake. I overheard a child scream and cry behind me. I noticed that he had all the safe bubbles on, life jacket, a blowout doughnut around his waist, and yet he was afraid to go in the lake. I learned several things that minute. The first, that it was my son's first time kayaking. And while he usually displays some type of reservation to do new things, he didn't this time. Was it because of his little friend, the perceived support? And lastly, some people, even with all the safety guards in the world, will still never experience new things, simply because they are scary. The question is, if you don't already have it innately (the fight in you), then can you acquire it? How else can that child be encouraged to try something new and scary for the first time? The peculiar thing is that what that child experienced was not unique to a child; it continues to occur to adults. And it happens with so much frequency that people begin to think it's part of their personality; they think it's part of who they are, when in reality it has been a perpetual habit reinforced by years of failing to confront fears. In a way, it is not their fault. It's simply a lack of training their mind to overcome.

So let me explain something in more detail. Originally I believed that motivation is like showering; it has to be done every day. Otherwise, it wears off. But in encountering leaders in my field and witnessing leadership today, I also realized that it may be innate in others. So the motivational/confidence showering thing doesn't work on all, or rather it is not needed in all people. As it happened to Isaac Newton, and his theory of gravity on that proclaimed apple falling off a tree, an apple also fell on me. This time in the form of Kevin Dutton's book *The Wisdom of Psychopaths*. He explains a lot about normal people and psychopaths. Why is this important? Because it explains traits that apparently are desired in leadership roles. And after all, we are looking to lead ourselves into a better life, career, and overall well-being. In his book he talks about a technique called transcranial magnetic stimulation or TMS, developed by Dr. Anthony Barker at University of Sheffield in 1985. In short, it is possible to modify the way the brain works when you alter the brain's electrical wiring. Essentially TMS combs your amygdala so that no electrical responses go through the area responsible for emotional and fear responses. In essence it numbs all the emotional and fear sensors in your brain so that you're more responsive to the "now" and become more insensitive. In fact in some of the interviews that Kevin Dutton did, people described themselves with a heightened sense of awareness of everything going on around them, "an intoxication that sharpens rather than dulls the senses."

Why do I mention the astonishing technique of TMS? Because Kevin Dutton himself went through a dose of the TMS, effectively making him understand what it was to be a psychopath, even if it was for thirty minutes.

> *"It isn't long before I start to notice a fuzzier, more pervasive, more existential difference... an easy, airy confidence. A transcendental loosing of inhibition...enhancement of attentional acuity and sharpness."*[3]

> —Kevin Dutton

See, if you are lacking leadership skills and traits that are more geared toward risk-taking, you are not alone. Most of us have that area of our brain

---

3   *The Wisdom of Psychopaths*. (2012). pg. 144-157.

that allows us to sympathize, care, and put our-selves in other people's shoes. However, with psychopaths, these traits that make them lethal, efficient, precise, and cold are part of their na-ture. The rest of us will have to practice and hone those skills that come naturally to them literal-ly every day. So what traits am I talking about? Let's see, charisma, self-confidence, the ability to influence, persuasive, visionary, risk-taking, action-oriented, and the ability to make hard decisions. I found that when I do slack off, it is like taking ten steps back. For me to get my edge back, my efficiency, I would have to re-engage in my craft and work at it again until it becomes second to none. But, as it is not natural for me, in essence, it is a perishable skill. Now what I am talking about here is not about becoming a psychopath, but rather learning to detach more from those crucial moments to get things done. Many of us overthink, are too afraid, or are too caught up in our own traumas and self-pity that we forego the experience that can take us a step closer to our desired state of happiness.

Please, don't go around electrocuting yourself. You are not alone. What's more, once you know where you are, you will know where to begin. It will take work, constant and persistent work. You are forging yourself, your best self; and only your vision of what you truly want to become will rise and reveal itself as you journey through it.

When I first was promoted to a supervisor, I knew I wanted it, and felt that I had all the necessary tools to excel. But I felt nervous and unsure of what exactly I needed to do. I had already been a field probation officer for a number of years. I had been trained in tactics, searching suspects, tactical communication, defensive tactics, and scenario training dealing with deadly force. I had been trained in dealing with the mentally ill and gang members. But this new promotion required a different me, a different set of skills. The very "unknown" factor as a new probation supervisor at juvenile hall was challenging. It was difficult to learn to shut off all emotional sensors at the time of crisis, and then when the suspect was controlled or in a place where he can be counseled and de-escalated, all your emotional and empathetic sensors have to turn back on. This happens so fast that there is no transitional time for an officer to think about what he/she needs to do next. When you show up on scene, all the officers literally stop and turn to look at you; even the inmate stops for a moment as if all of them are waiting for your instructions. You then have to make a decision. Oftentimes these decisions are hard and have to be made without regard of how you make people feel. That feeling thing only has a place afterward, when you debrief your staff.

So why was I at ease as a field probation officer but not as a supervising correctional officer? Simple, they are different environments, different expectations; one is a controlled environment (per se) and the other is not. As a field officer you only have your partner, and you are often confronted with a limited crisis, or one crisis at a time. As a supervising correctional officer, I was now in charge of approximately two hundred youths in custody and seventy custodial staff, including nurses, doctors, clinicians, therapists, custodians, parents, and other public servants coming in and out of the facility. The liability went up by multiple factors. Yeah, there was a reason to be nervous. Everyone is looking at your actions and the possibility of error in judgment with excessive force, treatment, equal rights, protection of rights, etc. As a field officer my judgment was mine alone; as a supervisor inside the facility, several officers and youths were the subject of attention. So, why the story? Just because I wasn't quite adept at this new task doesn't mean that I should have just quit. It meant that I had to work harder at it, understand where that fear was coming from, educate myself on the rules of the system I was now operating under, and then begin on self-improvement. Was it easy? Nope! Was it hard and sometimes downright scary? Yep! But, here is the kicker. We have to move way from "I want that promotion," "I want to lose weight," or "I would like that responsibility" to "I must make it happen." When we move from an "I wish" or an "I want" to a "must," we create magic. We create possibilities that we didn't think were possible. At that time I knew I wanted to reach the rank of sergeant, but at that moment, it was only a dream, especially with all the emotional limitations I felt I had. It wasn't until I began to work on what I had five feet ahead of me (figuratively speaking) that I became convinced the sergeant rank was possible and within reach.

On Self-improvement

Before we get further into practices, specific methods, and suggested exercises, let's first look at what we feed ourselves. While it is important to know what we feed our mind, who we hang out with, what thoughts we allow to soak into our very consciousness, and what negative and positive feedback we allow ourselves to believe, it is just as important to know what we feed our body. Lark and Richards's book *The Chemistry of Success* explains that the body uses 20 percent of the oxygen we inhale. Lack thereof contributes to aging and decline in memory and cognitive function. Two of many suggested solutions they provide are exercise and proper nutrition.

> *"Research studies done on adults who exercise on a regular basis compared with similar groups who are sedentary show striking differences in a variety of mental functions. Adults engaged in an active exercise program have better concentration and clearer and quicker thinking and problem solving abilities."*[4]

—The Chemistry of Success

So as you can see, it is not only a deep desire to excel that matters. It is also everything else you do for your mental and physical body. You can exhaust yourself, and at the end of the day you

---

4   Lark & Richards. *The Chemistry of Success*. p. 360-361.

will have nothing left to continue to get up every morning. A person with drive and determination can often outperform someone with natural talent. But this drive to excel often requires physical energy and stamina. And so the continuity of this sustained effort requires a great deal of energy. Is your lack of ambition a result of proper nutrition/oxygenation or lack of desire? If you are not already involved in some kind of physical activity on a routine basis, take the plunge and enroll in an activity. Commit yourself to two to three days a week for the first three to four weeks. Build the habit and then commit yourself to three to four times a week until you can sustain the effort to engage in physical activity five days a week. Take a look at what you eat, and educate yourself on what you put in your mouth. Just because it smells good, or just because it is what you grew up eating, it doesn't mean it's healthy or what you have to eat the rest of your life. Can you see the connection? Just because you grow up being beaten, it doesn't mean you have to continue to be beaten.

The goal is to reach a state where we can maintain focus and attain successful outcomes in times of stress. With a balanced diet, proper nutrition, and exercise, controlling emotional pain and tension surrounding difficult circumstances and decisions should be easier. Interestingly enough, author Anthony Robbins emphasizes the importance of aerobic exercises in creating the high level of physical energy needed for peak performance. In his book *Giant Steps*, he goes on to explain that having the physical energy required to sustain a high level of effort requires stamina.

We now know that proper nutrition, oxygenation, and exercise are key ingredients in your success formula. But that's not all. It is not only the physical body that needs to be fed. It is also the mind. We can wish all day long for what we want, what we want to become, what job we want, etc. But if at the end of the day we continuously sabotage our positive thinking with negative affirmations, where do you think we'll end up? You have to recognize where you are sabotaging yourself. When are you in a negative loop or negative behavior? You'll have to be on your constant guard so that you can stop the negative recording. We all have self-defeating thoughts that tell us why we can't do this or that, or why we are poor, why it's better to forego a promotion, etc. It all may be rooted deep in a traumatic experience, but it all starts with little things, like when we tell ourselves, "Oh, I hate mornings." Every day like a constant water drop, it will eventually carve out a dent in the rock, and so it will in your mind. Begin by identifying the feelings that support or justify your feelings of failure, and then address them, stop them, and tell yourself that there is no place for them in your mind. If need be, seek professional help. Remember, it's not just what you feed your body, it's what you feed your mind; and whatever the mind decides, the body will do. In fact Napoleon Hill, in his famous book *Think and Grow Rich*, goes on to explain how "whatever the mind can conceive and believe, the mind can achieve." To be more specific, scientists know that neuroplasticity is the ability of the brain to change throughout an individual's life. The older we get, the less neuroplasticity our brain has; hence our learning curves are longer, not shorter. In young children and adolescents, neuroplasticity is higher, hence their ability to learn things faster. Without getting into the whole science of it, and for the sake for simplicity, know that this too can be worked with. You can still learn new skills, but it will take you longer. Know that your habits have formed deep groves connecting neurons, i.e., habits. To change them will require you to begin new habits lasting longer, with more intensity, than the prior ones already there. Bottom line, you have a chance—if you stick with it, are consistent and diligent—to make them present in your daily routine.

Everything matters. Not one thing or another is exclusive but they are all mutually interdependent. So what's next? You're eating right, you're exercising, and you've cut your circle of friends to those who inspire you, motivate you, and fill you with enthusiasm. Okay, it's time to visualize your success. Earlier I talked about how I visualized wearing the black belt, and according to Marsha Sinetar in *Developing a 21st Century Mind*, there are several things you can do to inch yourself into achieving your goals.

After being a defensive tactics instructor for my bureau already for a number of years, late in 2013, I had been charged with reporting and analyzing the use of force for my division. This very specific assignment extrapolates data on officers' number of incidents where force was used to control, detain, and stop a suspect, and the reasons why. To make this as short as possible, the report goes deep into analyzing why the officers chose to use a specific control technique based on the "reasonableness standard." All that data has to be measured against legislative law and departmental policies and procedures. Although it was an ongoing assignment that never seemed to have an end, I realized that people had one basic deficiency when incidents were reviewed. Newer officers had difficulty grasping when to take action, how to identify a situation when it was about to escalate, and when to intervene. With my martial arts background and being a defensive tactics instructor, I realize that going through the motions is one thing, and beginning to visualize how an incident unfolds and taking action is another. I spoke to a number of my colleagues to determine if it was the actual training. But it wasn't. The department gave them plenty of training days, and under a controlled scenario environment, the new staff had an idea of what to do. I began to reflect on how I was able to overcome my fears when I first started with the department and how I mentally trained in martial arts. The answer was simple: teach them to visualize. This is a condensed version of what it all entails, what training the department teaches, and the concepts of use of force under the law. I'm keeping it short, but in all, the following email content is what started a series of training I was headed to teach:

How often do you visualize your success?

If you don't think this works, think again...

University of Chicago put this to the test. The final results... The brain doesn't know the difference between a real and an imagined experience.

To figure this out, they did two experiments:

1. When they asked a group of people to visualize a dog running, the recorded brain waves for the imagined and the real were identical.
2. They took three groups of kids. They told the first group to practice shooting a basketball for an hour a day, the second group they told to do nothing, and the third they told to visualize shooting and making the basket for one hour a day. Thirty days later... Guess what happened?

The first group improved by 24 percent.
The second group did not improve.
The third group improved by 23 percent.

Visualize running your unit with excellent structure, visualize counseling and de-escalating youths, visualize your success and how you want to carry it out when it's time to perform. Visualize walking into your unit and having fun, enjoying your job. If it works for the multimillion-dollar athletes, and it has been proven to work by science, why wouldn't it work for you?

For a series of weeks, I began to take small groups of officers, break down the concepts, and guide them through visualization exercises, from entering their living units, to counseling and de-escalating youths, to the application of control techniques. This is how athletes, martial artists, race car drivers, and yoga instructors do it. Why wouldn't it work for us?

Not exactly convinced yet? Let's take this a bit deeper. Roderick Gilkey and Clint Kilts published an article, "Cognitive Fitness," for the *Harvard Business Review*. Gilkey and Kilts explained the science behind the brain's learning capacity and the discovery of the brain's dedicated neural systems that represent objects, people, and actions. This dedicated neural system is made up of mirror neurons. They essentially help the brain speed up, with accuracy, how it perceives the world and its external experiences. In short, these mirror neurons help the brain learn through observation. The authors dub these mirror neurons as the brain's performance-enhancing neurons that accelerate learning and the capacity to learn. So what exactly do mirror neurons do? When you are shown how to do something, the mirror neurons supply the brain with a mental image of the action. Does this sound familiar when you visualize? You construct what you want, and your brain then goes to work and supplies the mental image. So, as in the experiment that University of Chicago did on the kids visualizing, when it was time to perform, the kids' brains had already "been there, done that." They had already rehearsed and practiced just as if it was real.

There is a cautionary note here, however (as in all '"surgeon general" advisory notes). Your visualizations and your desire to accomplish something have to be rooted deep, as in you have to have a burning desire within you to acquire it. In fact, you must almost taste it, touch it, and feel it. You have to practice your visualizations until they seem real, so real that you begin to expect your dream with enthusiasm; very much like how you know Christmas is coming. You have no doubt, you just know, and you're excited about it. You know your check is coming, so you don't worry if it's coming or not. You simply know, and you plan how you're going to save it or spend it. This is the type of expectation you must acquire.

Several years ago, while I was still in high school, my mother happened to "lend" me her book. The truth is that I still have it, and I never gave it back to her. She's even seen it on my bookshelf; but it's a treasure, it's hard to find, and it's out of print! I can't just let it go! So here it is. In U.S. Andersen's *Success Cybernetics*, he speaks about a great many things worthy of study (note how I say study, not just read), but there are only four things I want to emphasize. These four things have served me well, and once you study them, you too will realize how important they are. In fact, these four things can really be a game changer for you as they were for me. So without further ado:

You are what you concentrate on.
What you concentrate on seems real.
What you concentrate on grows.
You always find what you concentrate on.[5]

---

5   U.S. Andersen. *Success Cybernetics*. (1966) p. 29-31.

CHAPTER 5

On Acceptance

ACCEPTANCE FROM OTHERS is nothing more than an opinion on, an opinion usually formulated from a single event, maybe even a few events, but rarely in the totality or summation of the person. Therefore, gaining acceptance from others should never be a calculation of your worth. Your worth is only what you allow it to be.

Through the years of working for the department, I've come to see how this affects people. There was a guy, let's just say his name is Tom. Tom was ahead of his class, and he trained hard every day to master his craft. After several years of perfecting his expertise, he become known as the "expert trainer." One day he was involved in a situation where he helped fellow officers subdue a high-risk, violent offender who had already assaulted several other officers. In his field of expertise, he was able to gain control and manage the situation as best as anyone could have, under the same circumstances. However, the incident was forwarded to Professional Standards, or our department's equivalent of Internal Affairs. Tom was placed on administrative leave and sent home to wait until the department called him and made a decision. I cannot tell you exactly what occurred administratively, but I can tell you that he nearly lost his home and his car. After nearly a year, he was told to come back to work, with no discipline. For all intents and purposes, his case was closed and he came back to his job. There is one thing this man lost: his pride. This man had a military background; all he understood was chain of command, structure, discipline, orders, and as far as he knew, he followed all of them. So why did the very entity that he protected and honored doubt him? He felt betrayed; Semper Fi or Semper Fidelis (always loyal) no longer had meaning. And so the following days, weeks, and months, he showed up back to work absent, almost timid, and resentful.

When he was reassigned to my region, I had the

opportunity to converse with him. I asked him, "Why are you allowing the situation to control you? You're a Marine! And isn't it true that once a Marine always a Marine?" He smiled at me, and nodded with pleasure. I said, "Here is the thing, Tom, you can only control yourself, your actions, your thoughts, and your feelings; nothing more. When you attempt to control things outside of you, you will drive yourself crazy, you will experience disappointment, and eventually, you will be more dead than alive. All you can do is take several steps in the direction you think will get you where you want to go. Once you get there you will have to trust that next steps ahead of you will lead you to the right path. Tom, it's true we make a plan, and then work the plan, but in pursuing that plan all we take is educated guesses based on research, reading, and what others have done."

If things haven't worked out exactly as you mapped them, tweak your operating system, and adapt. Don't get stuck in the delusion that the world let you down, or that you weren't meant for this or that, or that people hate you. As you pursue your plan, try to live moment by moment so that you are aware of the experience. When you do this, you will be in "the zone." Your level of productivity rises, not because you became more intelligent overnight, but because your mind is ready to pay attention. When your mind is where it needs to be, it finds answers, it creates opportunity where there is none, it points out details you would have otherwise missed. You are who you are; do not allow a single event, or even a series of events, to deter you from what you love to do. The fear to engage will eat you alive, and when it's too late, you will ask yourself "Why did I do it to myself?" Tom, don't mistake the trees for the forest.

"From now on, then, resolve to live as
a grown-up who is making progress,
and make whatever you think best
a law that you never set aside."

—Epictetus, 135 AD

Whatever our resolve, we have to understand that events outside of us are not under our control. So it is not what happens to us, but what we choose to do with the things or circumstances that matters. If we don't get the promotion, the position, the new assignment, or the recognition, then it is up to us to re-examine the operating system. Did we compute the code wrong? Or is it simply out of control?

We work endless hours, we put ourselves last, we put our families last, our time, and so that in the end, our efforts are passed by and are not rewarded or recognized. Sound familiar? That's because this is very real. It isn't so much that these people have done something wrong, as much as it is setting their priorities right and understanding why they do what they do. My father would always tell me, "Do what you love, and love what you do." Later on I caught this phrase again reading Dale Carnegie, where he elaborated that when you do this, you end up delivering more than you are asked for. Why? Because work is no longer work, its pleasure, a passion that you get excited about. When you do this, the form of payment becomes enrichment, and you do eventually get paid more than you ask for. Now when I first read this, I must have been in my early twenties. Not much of this made sense, but over the years I've seen colleagues repeatedly get discouraged, and I realized that the enrichment you get out of your work depends largely on knowing why you do what you do and loving it!

I'd often ask my discouraged colleagues, why are

you doing this? I mean, you're in law enforcement to be an agent of change, to help others when they can't help themselves, to aid, protect, and show compassion where there is none. They'd usually reply, well...yeah. So why are you allowing someone's opinion that you aren't ready for a promotion affect you? You are still an agent of change! And isn't that why you started to begin with? It was a reminder that the reward for being in the profession was not to get a promotion, but to be an agent of change. It was an intrinsic motivation.

We are not dependent upon someone's opinion of us for self-worth. It's not even about being in law enforcement. You could be in sales, in the plumbing business, real estate, etc. The bottom line is that when you hear a "no," you should really be hearing a "yes." Don't give up, and never lose sight of why you chose that path, the career, the job, etc. If you can't honestly remember why or whether you love what you do, then it is time for a reassessment; it is time to re-inventory your life, your priorities, and what you need to do next.

Harry F. Harlow in the 1960s conducted experiments involving motivation using monkeys as his test subjects. In short, he found that there was a drive he called "intrinsic motivation," meaning behavior that seeks rewards from the task itself, and when rewards are added to complete a task, more errors occur and performance actually decreases, when all other things are held constant (meaning these monkeys were not starving and all other biological needs were met). Now these were monkeys, and one should suggest that these primates are far less sophisticated than we are. I had come across this study early on in my sociological classes in college. Years later Daniel H. Pink wrote *Drive; The Surprising Truth About What Motivates Us*. In the opening chapter he mentions another gentleman by the name of Edward Deci. Deci picked up where Harlow left off, and instead of using monkeys for test subjects, he used people. He divided people into two groups and set the stage for what results in the same outcome as what Harlow arrived at. Essentially, what this suggests, in our context, is that in your pursuit for success; do not focus on the outcome. Focus on what you have at hand. So why regurgitate this study? Because you should be focusing on the "game," on loving what you do, and doing what you love. This will produce the results you want, often as it is translated into money, wealth, fame, and abundance of what you seek. Money, the external reward, only serves its purpose as a jolt of caffeine, but doesn't last long. The reward for doing what you do every day should really come from a deeper place inside you. Forget about the money; focus on your passion, on your intrinsic motivation. The money will come to you as a side effect, proportionate to your passion and the love for what you do.

In this case we talk about money as the external reward, but in reality there are several other external rewards. We often get sidetracked by these rewards and soon forget about what brought us to that place to begin with. Daniel H. Pink mentions two types of people with different behaviors toward what motivates them. The first is Type I behavior, or rather a person motivated intrinsically, as mentioned above. The second is Type X behavior, or a person motivated by external—extrinsic—rewards. Really at the end of the day, it depends on you knowing yourself. Again, if you are motivated by intrinsic rewards, but you allow people to push you to be motivated by extrinsic rewards, you will not succeed, you will not be happy, and you will be miserable. The same is true for the reverse. Often you will hear people say "What's in it for me?" Remember that the external reward is not often money. It could be a promotion, power, authority, prestige, or bragging rights. The cautionary tale here is, don't dismiss the third drive. Pink explains, "Our innate need to direct our own lives, to learn and create things, and to do better by ourselves and our world."

Allow me to take a step back for a moment. Years ago, early in my teens I had the opportunity to live in Mexico City. Coming from Southern California, sunny San Diego, it was a shock to me. While I did see many good people, I also saw not-so-good people. People's motivation in places like that come from a different place. In many instances I witnessed that success was not attained by an intrinsic motivation, but rather to simply fulfill a biological desire, mainly where basic necessities were lacking or nonexistent. Here is where Maslow's hierarchy triangle comes in. There was no doubt that poverty in this city was caused by fierce competition for jobs, and lack of government aid, housing, and food shortages. The list goes on, but the important thing here is that people's motivation was to fulfill a basic need, like food, shelter, clothing, and procreation. I saw people living under bridges and building their homes out of cardboard, from aluminum pieces, and generally from whatever they could find. At one point, I realized that one of my classmates actually lived in a cave with his family. This is something you don't see every day in San Diego, California. Even in these environments you still see the very successful people acting on intrinsic motivation. Most people who were considered successful in my neighborhood would often give advice to the youths, telling them that you have to love what you do, because when you do, people like your work and then business comes to you. Makes sense, sort of like how "word of mouth" works. Although these people few and far between, lacking the basic necessities, they existed nonetheless. Perhaps statistically speaking, they were "outliers"; they were neither here nor there and did not make up the majority of the population in a bell curve.

Efforts

Earlier we mentioned the 10X rule authored by Grant Cardone: double your efforts, assess where that takes you, and double your efforts again. In time and through purpose and intent, you will be able to sustain efforts ten times more than your competition and yourself as Grant Cardone suggests. Let's take a moment to write down an event or a series of events where you had to push your-self beyond what you thought you could. Write about at least two, and elaborate on the event, retell your story, step by step if you have to. Work on this story for five or ten minutes every day for a week. Then set it aside for two days and then go back to it. Read your story, identify where you exerted beyond your limits, and where you had to step outside your box. This event or series of small events can be academic, in sports, in re-lationships, or of a spiritual nature. There is no right and wrong answer; the only requirement is for you to re-examine your life. Once you can identify how this occurred, you can duplicate the effort, and then double it.

When I re-examined the long court battle, I can-not honestly tell you that I had everything under control, or that I knew somehow the outcome. I was not conscious that I was going to have to work ten times more than my opposition. My drive was different, but the outcome proved that I did work ten times harder than what my op-position thought possible. My passion and my desire had to be greater than anything else. I slept very little, I hustled for extra shifts, and had to think every day how I was going to nourish my body. I knew I couldn't sustain that intense effort on nothing. I looked to "super foods," vitamin B injections, meditation, listening to subliminal suggestions, listening to frequencies. I tried it all, and I did it all every day. If I was to sustain a battle that required ten times my effort, I knew I had to nourish and exert my body and mind ten times more. I saw beyond winning; I set my target beyond that. I projected my opposition simply coming to me and giving up, telling me that they no longer wanted to fight me in court, and that all my demands would be agreed to. I had accepted all possibilities, including losing. But in spite of this, my desire to ensure that my son had a father to raise him had to be beyond my comfort zone. I could not take "no" for an answer, and so failure, although acknowledged, was not an option.

"There is no reason to suffer. The only reason you suffer is because you choose to suffer...The same is true for happiness. The only reason you are happy is because you choose to be happy."[6]

—Miguel Angel Ruiz, M.D.

---

6   Miguel Angel Ruiz, M.D. *The Four Agreements.* (1997) pg. 139.

I started out my mornings by playing my favorite motivational speaker on my iPod. I'd do a few sets of calisthenics, shower, and eat breakfast—nothing processed, nothing sugary, no salts. I then would put on my best clothes. I once read, "Don't dress like you're getting a loan from a bank; dress like you own the bank." I don't know where this came from or who said it, but it certainly made sense. If you feel good, and people see you well dressed, the likelihood of being treated well goes up exponentially. My father died well dressed. In his life he believed that his presentation was his duty. His best friend Jim would ask him, "What's the occasion?" My father would say, "Jim, you deserve to see me at my best." At first I really thought that he meant always a tie and suit, but now I realize that it's not the tie or the suit; it's simply your best. When people see you at your best, they naturally want to be around you; they assume that you are in control, that you are somehow trustworthy. Somehow we assume that if people are well put together, then they must have their lives "put together." In so many ways, this can be so deceiving. But for the purpose of empowering yourself, it is another resource. It's part of the equation; you're going to war, you must put on your armor. So don't bring a knife to a gunfight.

Every minute I had free at work I would divide my time in four. The first was to take time for my staff and my "walkabout" (which we will talk about later), and then I would take a book and read. The third was for work and so I would take time to study the department's policies and procedures. The fourth would be for journaling five to ten minutes. After work would be exclusively for hitting the gym, treadmill, or a run. I was a madman, but you kind of have to be when you are making success not only your responsibly, but your mission. Now success can be many different things to people. Success is even situational to events, times, and people. If you're looking to pass an exam, studying and preparing, passing the exam will be considered a success. For many success is not a matter of passing an exam; perhaps it is getting a promotion, getting a job, buying your first home, etc. The point is that you have to set your goals, set benchmarks so you know how you are progressing, and then track how you are succeeding. Most importantly, success is a choice, a personal responsibility, and it should be your mission. When you take responsibility to be successful, you will no longer make excuses and you will overcome the "what if's," anxiety, and doubt.

Fight the Fight

I can remember going to the gym for the first time. I was about 135 pounds—a skinny rail. I walked in only to find myself surrounded by muscle heads, aficionados who looked like they belonged on a cover of a magazine. I walked through the racks of weights, machines, and endless rows of people who seemed to know what they were doing. So where do you start? Set a goal, make a plan, and work the plan. For this to happen, as in any new endeavor, you must do research, network, talk to people, read. Once that is established, you now have to contend with something bigger—your thoughts. They will play tricks on you, they will tell you that you can't, and try to convince you why you are wasting your time. Your job is to get yourself fired up, and tell yourself to forget about what others are doing and get your butt in the gym. You keep track of your workouts, when you go, what you eat, and recovery times. This basic formula is surprisingly no different than anything else you want to accomplish.

I can still remember sitting in my car, frozen with fear, anxious because I was allowing my mind to convince me that the gym wasn't for me. But if you want something you've never had, you must do things you've never done. Simple, right? Well, it is easier said than done. I've mentioned before the freeze, flight, or fight syndrome. Too many of us get stuck in the car, not wanting to get out, frozen; and yet for others, they will even take flight or run. They will leave convinced by their pet complexities that they are not worth the change they want. You have to fight your thoughts. The reality is that no one cares inside that gym, no one, so you must get in there and do your thing! This of course is only an example, but the same principle applies to everything else. There will always be naysayers, haters, or back stabbers, but they don't really care. It's only a fleeting moment of judgment and emotion that comes and goes; who cares! Your job is to keep showing up and to work your ass off!

Allow me to take you back when I was still married to my second wife. I was coming in to work after everyone knew that she was an addict and was under investigation by the department, and rightly so. Showing up to work, I knew there was gossip, I knew there were rumors, and frankly some of the people I knew no longer wanted to associate with me; and rightly so again. But my job was not to give credence to their perception, or to attempt to convince them that I was not involved. My job was to get in there, kick ass, work harder than anyone else, and keep showing up. The truth of the matter is that no one really cared, so I couldn't get hung up on my feelings or what others thought of me. I needed to do me, and doing me had to take priority. It is in those moments that you have to recognize when your mind and your body are freezing. You then must take back control of yourself, of your anxious body that refuses to move, and move it, little by little, until you are at the door walking in.

Every day my goal was to not call off work, and actually walk in. When I did, I'd pat myself on my back and congratulate myself for that small success. Every time I did that, I knew I was overcoming my freeze, flight, fight syndrome. The more I did it, the easier it became until it was no longer a struggle. It worked the same way for the gym; and it will work the same way in everything else. In order to beat this "freeze," you have to be conscious, aware of what is happening; a moment-by-moment awareness. Ask yourself, is this real? Am I making this up? Is what I perceive as a threat a real threat? Rationalize it and take its power away; it has no room in your head, and no place in your mind. Your body will do what your mind tells it to do, but if your mind is caught up in mind games, it will freeze. Try to input conflicting commands on a computer program and it will do the same; it will freeze. Refer back to your plan, stick to your plan, and continue to push through until that plan becomes a habit. Eventually you will look like a "natural," a "prodigy," but under close scrutiny people will see that it was hard work, dedication, and a consistent worked plan.

Incidentally enough the flight syndrome works the same way, and so does the fight in you. These three perils (freeze, flight, fight) are perishable skills; and so practicing them is absolutely necessary. Consider it your personal responsibility, your duty, your ethical obligation; and watch how your life begins to change.

The Fight Never Stops, It Just Changes

In late October of 2016, I was involved in a car accident. I was the passenger in the front seat. The traffic was heavy and came to a stop. The afternoon was hot, and after a long day at work I couldn't wait to get home. Just as my coworker and I were stopping with traffic, an SUV rear-ended us at what seemed about forty or fifty miles per hour. The following days, weeks, and months led to physical therapy. The first three months were awful. I couldn't get up, I couldn't pick things up, and I was on pain medication. The worst thing was that with a newborn in the house, I couldn't even help carry my new daughter or bathe her. What made things worse was living in the mountains. And if you have been in the mountains, you realize that it involves stacking wood, chopping wood, snow, rain, and mud. I love the mountain life, but with an injury, it proved really difficult at every turn.

I had to fight the fight again; this time it was against me. Now here in this situation I had to really talk to myself every day, cheer myself up, fire myself up every day, and keep both my body and my mind sharp. Especially after the spine specialist told me that the injury may be lifelong, to expect pain for the rest of my life, and, in his own words, "You may have to consider another profession." Quite frequently I'd ask myself, "How the hell did this happen? And why in the hell did it happen to me?!"

We all ask ourselves these questions at one point or another, but it always seems like we are alone in our journey and we act as if we are the only ones to ever go through this. The truth is that there are a lot of us who have this type of challenge. In fact we may go through a series of challenges throughout our lives. Each challenge prepares us for the next, so that we may overcome it. The perplexing question is why some people never get back up, while others do. If you look at each individual, you'll see that they just refuse to stay down, and have no doubt in their mind that they will. This is not to say that they don't ever have doubts, but they work through them actively, consciously. This is no easy feat, and it wasn't for me either. By late 2018, I was back on my feet; it took me over a year, with constant physical therapy, paying attention to what I ate, and being diligent what I fed my mind. It was tiring because I knew it had to be done every day; quitting wasn't allowed. I knew that if I wanted to be back on my feet, I needed to push myself further, and then double my efforts. I reread all my books, kept my affirmations current, and recited them daily, up to three to four times a day.

While there was no quitting allowed, rest days were as important as the workdays themselves. Just like in any process, the recovery is crucial, especially if you are overcoming large obstacles in your life. These recovery sessions are to be taken seriously and at intervals in your training. Too many recovery sessions and you lose the "heat of the moment." Prolong recovery sessions and you lose the fire in your drive. But without the recovery sessions, you won't know what your fire is about, and the "why" drifts off into the distance. Have you ever experienced firsthand getting so upset and so angry at someone but after years or months, you forget the reason why you were so angry to begin with? Again, don't miss the forest for the trees.

Things can get tricky and downright exhausting, so keep a journal. There is a reason why athletes and bodybuilders keep logs of their performance and their food intake. They keep records of their present limitations, not so that they can dwell in it, but so that they can surpass it. For bodybuilders, it's called "progressive overload." If you are a bodybuilder or weight lifter, you know that the purpose of this is for the body to grow and to force the body to recruit more muscle fibers to be able to lift a heavier load. There is no difference in how we deal with our challenges. We must keep our body, spirit, and emotional selves in shape so that when life demands an "overload," our body in its entirety can recruit and force itself to handle this progressive overload.

My son at the time had just turned seven years old. The prior year he had participated in the school's annual talent show, where he was among several other kids, signing and following prompts. The year he was seven years old, however, he memorized a poem two pages long. He had committed the poem to memory and practiced at home, at school, and in front of his classmates for two weeks. It seemed like he had it under control. On the day of, he got dressed with brand-new shoes, a favorite blazer and tie. He looked the part and very handsome. As we walked to the car and into the auditorium, he walked with an air of confidence as he swayed his shoulders. He walked past his friends as the schoolgirls and parents were awed at his composure. As I followed behind him I could not help but think that he was already better than I at his age; his composure was miles from mine at seven. The first act came and went, and finally on the fourth act it was his turn. He stood up and walked onto the podium. He stood in silence with the prompts behind him, and then there was nothing. You could see a sudden realization in his eyes. It was real now, and he was not expecting that reality. As his teachers began to encourage him, he began to cry. After several minutes he sat back down. Two more acts came and went, and he again attempted it. He stood up and this time walked onto the podium with his best friend. No luck again. He froze even with encouragement from his family and teachers. Again he sat down. After that he could not work up the courage to do it, and so the talent show ended.

My first instinct was to reprimand my son and to ground his little butt for quitting—a concept that our family had drilled in him. But...on second thought, if I wanted to reinforce a behavior, then continuous exposure was necessary until his fear was gone. Therefore, I told him that I was proud of him for getting on stage, not once, but twice. I told him that we would work on getting him out of stage fright. Likewise, if you have suffered "paralysis" in your life, don't run, don't hide. What you need is guided exposure, until what you fear becomes a thing of the past. Without guided exposure, gained experience, and without a plan, you will never get over fears. And so practiced "progressive overload" will enable you to take life's demands in stride. You can overcome this flight, fight, and freeze peculiarity.

Has that happened to you? Of course it has, maybe not on a podium, but at meetings when you know you need to speak up, but you don't. It happens when your spouse says something that upsets you, but you don't set boundaries. It happens when your father, mother, uncles, aunts, or guardians put you down and you take it. Why?

During my undergraduate studies at University of Redlands, I learned about customs in various cultures as part of my sociology and anthropology studies. One particular custom was when older men would offer cattle to a family in exchange for their daughters, often underage. In those parts of the world, it's a practice that is acceptable. But here is the kicker: once the arrangement was made, the small child would be told to "take it. There are cattle." If you haven't read between the lines, here is what happens. My mother, when she was first married to my biological father, hated the idea of being married to him, a forced marriage. Young as she was, fifteen, this man was only a few years older at twenty. Often she would cry to her mother that she wasn't happy. What was her mother's reply? "You have a car, a house, a maid, and a husband that will do anything for you. Take it." In her own native language it was "aguantate" (to endure it).

Fast-forward to today, and we all just "take it" for the promise of a cow in the future, or because "it pays the bills." Why do we sacrifice our right to be human, to be free, for the promise of a cow that perhaps we will never get, see, or enjoy? When it wasn't our dream to begin with?

With Wisdom, you realize the fight was never a fight

When you fast-forward into the future, you can "see" that you are a better person because of what you have gone through. In fact, most people, as in my case, would say they wouldn't change a thing about what they experienced. That the experience has made them who they are, strong willed, and has given them a sense of appreciation and gratefulness in their lives. But often, in the middle of it, in the "thick of it," we won't see it; not because we don't want to, but because all our senses are being recruited to deal with the situation beforehand.

Mistakes do not exist as long as there is a progressive realization of awareness. If there is no progressive realization of awareness, the person gets stuck in a loop, and by the law of attraction, if you believe; you will continue to attract what you concentrate on, what you think about most of the time. This is why in looking back at our lives; we can see that some situations were for the best. But ever wonder how some people get "stuck" and are the same way they were five, ten, fifteen years ago? This is why you often hear that mistakes are learning lessons. No doubt, some lessons are harsh, even more challenging than others. As long as you can examine what occurred and take a correction action plan, then mistakes are lessons, not mental and emotional prison sentences.

CHAPTER 6

Timed Success...The Clock is Ticking

TIME—EVERYONE WANTS IT, no one can catch it, it's mesmerizing, and its elegance seduces. Most people are always chasing what they believe they can't have. They look at the time and think, "I don't have time" or "There just isn't enough time to get it done..." Somehow there is a belief that time directly manipulates our ability for success. Success isn't something that you "get," because if it was, you'd probably head down to the local mom-and-pop shop and buy yourself a box of success. But you can't, and for a reason. Success is like your freedom—it's up to you to exercise it, to summon it from within, and through your imagination and intellect create it. Here is the exciting thing about success: it's free to take, and it exists in so much abundance that there is enough for everyone. What success creates varies in quality and quantity, and most often it yields returns in terms of money, but not always. So let's define success.

My father would drill into me this definition. I don't know where he heard it or who originally said it, but over the years it made sense. Success isn't just about money or a house, a boat, or a promotion, and although many people categorize these things as success with certainty, they are not. They are merely a byproduct of what they actually intended to create. Every time I received a promotion, my father would ask me, "Why? What were you after?" I would contemplate the question, and my first responses would always be because I wanted to earn more money. But once I really studied the questions, I would realize that the reasons were more altruistic, more intrinsic. I wanted to make a change. I wanted to contribute more, and the promotion simply allowed me access to contribute more. Now contribution wasn't always the intrinsic value; it was also self-fulfillment, self-realization, and self-mastery. It was about gaining access to more freedom, financial or otherwise. The money from the promotions was a byproduct, though it always seemed like everyone brought it up first in conversations. I'd bet even the chief, if asked, would give an altruistic answer for her success, and not even suggest it was about money.

So what is success? Success is a progressive realization of a worthy ideal. Why define success? Because if success is a worthwhile dream worth pursuing in your life, then the "gold nuggets" we've been talking about all this time create a formula, and you'll be surprised how simple that formula really is. Again, don't miss the forest for the trees. At the end of the day, some concepts will serve you well, while others won't. Just like a tool set, not all jobs require a hammer. You have to have a repertoire that you can refer to, like looking at your map when you are not sure where you are going. The map won't get you to your destination; it is merely a guide. Whatever you can use, you use, and everything else is irrelevant until it becomes relevant. "Magic books" or "magic seminars" exist, but they are only partial functions of the total sum of success that will teach you all you need to know. Have you ever attended seminars where you come out so pumped that you feel invincible? If you haven't attended one, attend one—they are magical—but always remember that motivation is like showering: it wears out and needs to be done every day, and this is why I say motivation is not permanent. Motivation needs maintenance, much like your car, only more consistent and more frequent. The truth is that it all lies inside you already; it's your desire, your focus, your wants, your love, your attention to what you want. You will then find what you concentrate on and bring it into reality. Hence, you will learn to see the opportunities that will bring you closer to what you want. But whatever it is, always love what you do, and do what you love. If it is a means to an end, it is all right as long as you hold yourself accountable and move toward your goal every day, no excuses.

$$ Money, Money, Maaa...noey $$...!

So far we've talked about the magic of things, and the byproduct of doing what you love, and loving what you want. We've even talked about forgetting about the byproduct and focusing on where your passion lies. Here is the thing: money does matter, and it matters a lot. So why did we say to forget the money? Because the focus of your happiness needs to have clarity. Money is a construct of our society; it has weight and value only because the majority of our institutions have deemed it necessary. It's a modern bartering system, a means to an end; you essentially trade goods and services for it. So by deductive reasoning, money only serves to acquire what you truly desire.

Furthermore, money is a major factor in the divorce rate in the U.S., and it is also a major contributor to mental health problems like anxiety, depression, and even suicide. You have to have money to eat, drive, house yourself, and clothe yourself. Yes, it is important, and oftentimes people will ask, "How can I do what I love when I have bills to pay, and the job I have pays the bills?" There are simple ways to do this; pay your debt off! If you can't control your debt, get rid of the credit cards and try to pay for things with cash. If you don't have enough cash to pay for what you want, then you don't need it. Now, you can either invest your money, or you can spend less once you free yourself from debt. Here I am not claiming to be a financial advisor, but these simple rules are essentially universal; get rid of your overhead. Most financial advisors will even tell you to invest in some type of retirement. That decision will be entirely up to you, although highly advisable, but what you choose to invest in will be up to you. So how important is it to get yourself free from modern slavery? Well, according to the Federal Server, 80 percent of Americans today are in debt, and on average, most Americans have about $8,000 in consumer debt. Sure, there are ways to build wealth, but that is not a topic of discussion today. The main focus is that you need to prioritize your life, set yourself free from debt, and begin to live your life.

Abracadabra

Earlier I mentioned that we must hold ourselves accountable for our success, our goals, our dreams. This is much more than that, however. I mentioned a few techniques on how to hold yourself accountable, but what this really means is that you must treat your word as the ultimate contract. My father used to tell me—well, actually he would preach constantly, "Giovannelli, be authentic!" Over the course of conversations what he really meant to say is that being authentic means being honest with yourself; and being honest with yourself means to control your words. Every time my father would ask me to mow the lawn, I'd say, yes! It'll be done, no problem. A fifteen-year-old hardly understands the power of his word. When my father would return home from work, before he could even change clothes, he'd walk to my room and ask, "What happened, Giovannelli? You gave me your word that you'd mow the lawn." I'd usually come up with excuses, even homework and school. He then would go into a long monologue about how it is not about what we think is more important. It is about accountability for what you say, to yourself and others. Can your word have that much power? Of course it can. People can believe that they have days or weeks left to live, and they will self-fulfill the prophecy. Even if we don't go to such extremes, when a child is repeatedly told that they are not good at something, or are repeatedly insulted, that child will grow up believing the abusive behavior; power of words can influence to the degree that people can be held slaved to lies. I've been in the field of "rehabilitating" young adolescents, and I can tell you that in fifteen years I have yet to see otherwise. Words have the power to keep you down and to motivate you. Choose your words wisely, and, more importantly, choose who you listen to.

"The word is not just a sound or a written symbol. The word is a force; it is the power you have to express and communicate, to think, and thereby to create the events in your life."[7]

—Miguel Angel Ruiz, M.D.

The promise you have to make to yourself should be to practice and have impeccability of your word so that every agreement you have and every promise you make to yourself is fulfilled. This is success, when you can make a statement to yourself, a promise, and fulfill your dreams through a consistent realization of a worthwhile dream. What will you choose, to live as a bystander or to live your life as the best version of yourself? Your intent is always manifested through your word, and then action. Even the word you say in silence to yourself repeatedly has an impact on your subconsciousness. Everything counts, but you have to pay attention to it. If you read the Bible, or any other religious or spiritual text, you'll find the importance of honoring and keeping your word. You are the most important person you have to keep promises for, so be authentic. Don't waste

---

7   Miguel Angel Ruiz, M.D. *The Four Agreements.* (1997). p. 30.

your time on promising things you won't do or can't fulfill.

> *"Before you speak, let your words*
> *pass through three gates:*
> *Is it true?*
> *Is it necessary?*
> *Is it kind?"*

—Rumi, 13th Century Persian Poet

Masaru Emoto researched in his book *Messages from Water* how the environment influences water, its quality, and contamination issues. He did this by photographing water crystals when subjected to sounds, music, and voices. In short, it demonstrated that if polluted water is filtered every possible way, it will remain with its pollutants, with its unstable structure. In a few words, the frozen crystallized water served like a memory, much like a computer saves data on its hard drive. What was more interesting is that as the water was subject to different "intentions" (good, kind, loving, bad, anger, etc.), the crystallized water demonstrated a well-structured crystal, or a distortion; sometimes a nonexistent crystal. You have to see it to believe it, but the purpose is for you to realize that the sounds (words), along with the intent (feeling) behind the words have a direct impact even on the very water we drink and consume. Imagine what happens when you are hateful to yourself, your life, and everything you are while you drink water and eat? You are essentially changing the very sustenance you eat and drink to benefit you or destroy you.

You are composed of approximately 80 percent water, so the sound (word), followed by intent (feeling), can empower you or hinder your progress. This is why we mention affirmations, knowing who you get advice from, who you listen to, and who you hang out with. This matters because if you are around toxic people long enough, they will contaminate you, your desire to achieve, and most importantly, your belief in yourself to be and have everything and anything you want. Remember, it is not merely enough to recite like a parrot a set of affirmations. Your words have to have intention, feeling behind them, for them to have power, for them to have "magic."

Play Time

When you feel stuck, or you think you're stuck, it's time to take a walk. Previously I had spoken about a "walkabout." During my studies for the graduate program of master's in Business Administration, I learned about what is known to management as a walkabout. It's simply a practice of getting out of your office and talking to employees; it's considered a form of cognitive exercise. I learned about this when I read a case study on Xerox, where Anne Mulcahy, CEO of Xerox at the time, sought advice from Warren Buffett. The advice was simple: do a walkabout, interact with your environment, and learn what it needs, how it breathes, how it plays, how it interacts with others.

George S. Clason, author of *The Richest Man in Babylon*, talks about financial cures, specifically the "Fifth Cure": make of thy dwelling a profitable investment. When we "own" our actions, our responsibilities, our work, we place care in it, we are proud of it, we "putteth" confidence in our heart and greater effort behind all our endeavors. Although Clason speaks of owning your own domicile, it is hard to ignore what's behind his words. We oftentimes spend more time at work than at home. In some cases by choice, others by default. Nevertheless, many simply go through the motions, never really "owning it," and instead complain about why success hasn't really approached them. How silly that is, yet many of us get stuck in that mind-set. It is not up to success to come to us; it is up to us to develop it, deicide on it, and then own it as if it was our home. After all, you are building your foundations, your supporting beams, the frame on which your success will stand. It's your house, your building, so make it strong and profitable as Clason puts it; and by profitable we mean secure, stable, peaceful, rich, and abundant.

When you get stuck, do a walkabout of your "house." For all intents and purposes, the house we speak of is all your dreams, what you are working on, your marriage, your kids, perhaps even your actual workplace. Whatever is at the forefront for you, that is your house. As you do your walkabout, think of what your house needs, how it works, what it eats! Does it thrive on people, things, physical space, and stats? The measurement of success differs from industry to industry, even more so from person to person. There is a reason why it is said that there is enough for everyone, because not everyone wants what you want.

As you discover what your house needs, remember to play with it. Ease your mind so that if you are a thinker, consider that sometimes the numbers won't add up; you just have to trust that they will. If you are a feeling type person, then do! If you are a doer, stop to ponder what you do have. You have to get into an uncomfortable place where you are forced to see a different perspective of your problem.

One particular and deep concept that Clason speaks of is of freedom, though seemingly related to a more altruistic form. He tells of a tale of a free man who through mismanagement of financials became a slave. He learned a few things from others as he was traded from owner to owner. Eventually he ended up serving the wife of a wealthy man. One day the wife asked the slave to gather the camels and fetch them, get them ready for a trip to see her mother, not too distant, but he wondered why pack them with so much? As they finally arrived at their destination, the wife urged the slave to take off and leave. She would say he escaped. The slave looked puzzled and froze. She then asked him, "If not a slave, what are you?"

Isn't a slave always a slave? He will always find it necessary to be a slave, always give in to excuses, give in and give up his right to be free; his freedom of choice and responsibility to those who choose freedom.

What a profound concept! It is easier to give it up than to take responsibility for it. For true freedom requires active participation; it requires that you pay attention to what you do every day, and that you are careful not to misuse it, mistreat it, or take it for granted. Use your freedom wisely, but remember that it is yours and yours alone to summon, believe in, and act upon. Freedom, like money and health, doesn't just appear; you have to decide on it.

Desire

So in learning to secure that one thing, that one desire to set yourself on the path to your success, you must decide how you are going to get there. Be careful not to start the impractical or difficult task. It's important that once you determine what you are seeking, you hone in on priorities. Start like a snowball effect, each subsequently building on the next, learning and becoming more capable each time. This will allow you to reach the bigger goals/dreams while increasing your confidence. This is the same process of how to get out of debt, how to build up your savings account, how to build more wealth. You can't do algebra without first knowing the basics of math. Desire can be anything as big or little as you like. There is no limit, but how can you begin to cross off your checklist of things you want to accomplish? Desire, like goals, must start out definite and simple. So begin with asking what you want. For sake of conversation let's say you want to exercise common sense. This is broad because common sense mean many things to many people. So ask, what is it about common sense that you would like to address? According to a basic search on the web on the definition of common sense, it is a noun: "good sense and sound judgment in practical matters." So what you are really seeking is better decision making. Then branch out what you need in terms of resources, people, things, and how you are going to get there. These methods are not applicable universally, and they will also differ from person to person. You will have to know and understand what type of person you are. That of course will require you to take action. Are you a thinker, a person who feels, a doer, or a person who jumps off the cliff and asks question as you are headed down to the ground? Understand that there is nothing wrong with you, so you'll just have to understand what method works best for you. Once you decide on what methods, you'll have to begin to apply them to see how it works out, and adjust in the process. Remember that adjusting and readjusting doesn't mean you are quitting your purpose. The desired result is still in your sights. It's how you need to navigate to get there that might require you to steer, do a turnabout, do a U-turn if you over-shoot your mark, or even stop to reassess.

Think about how you or others around you talk about goals and dreams, and how they are going to accomplish this or that, but never get any-where. Then at New Year's, they are making the same resolution as the last year. It's simple, make a plan, and work the plan.

The Walkabout

Years ago when I was in college, I worked with my first wife's grandfather as a used car salesman. He had his locale in a small town, and at that time he was close to his seventies. By all accounts he had attained success. His house was paid off, his wife didn't have to work, they went on cruises every other month, and generally lived a healthy life. He owned his dealership of about ten to fifteen cars on the lot ranging in price from about 2k to 14k. The bulk of sales were the low-end commuter cars; and he did in-house financing for those with a bad credit score or those who were trying to restore their credit. Oftentimes you'd see him doing walkabouts on his lot. You'd think, a lot that small, why would you need to do a walkabout? But as it turned out, every time he did one, he'd come back inside the office excited and with a new idea. "Let's put up a new billboard," or "Let's rearrange all the cars by color, size, price, or year model." He always had me doing something. And while I sometimes found it tiresome and useless, it gave him the spark and creativity he needed to sell. He would say, "I know just the right person for the car. I'm going to call him now."

As he would go through this day in and day out, one day I asked him, "How did you get here, and did you always know?" He said to me, "If you can remember one thing, remember this: have a plan, and work the plan." He then went on to tell me that he really didn't know what he wanted in the beginning, but he knew he had a love for cars and he loved to talk to people. At the time he was barely a high school graduate. He then began to work for a dealership. He would tell stories of triumph, big sales, of months where he would sell in volumes; and then there were months that there were no sales and his family had to go without money. Of how his wife would make miracles happen and make the little they had last them longer. He would save every penny, dime, and nickel, and forego "consumer expenses." I'd ask him, "Like what?" His answer was "Anything that requires a payment. If you can't buy it with cash, you can't really afford it. I'd stop and think, *How is that possible?* I mean, everyone needs a car, a mortgage, and student loans. He would finish his Danish, wipe the crumbs, and say, "Don't mistake the forest for the trees. It's about priorities, knowing what you want, making a plan, and working that plan—that simple. Don't overcomplicate things. If you don't have a clue what you want, you'll waste a lot of money, time, and energy; you'll end up being jack of all trades and master of none. With a lot of debt and misdirection."

This man cleared between 12k and 15k a month without even trying. A millionaire? Maybe not, but he didn't have to be. He found his area of contentment, his happiness, and his freedom. He lived by very basic principles; he had a plan and worked the plan. The rest he didn't really worry about. And every day he simply showed up, again and again and again. Did he suffer at times financially? Was he ever short on money, food, or basic necessities? I'm sure he was, but he had to readjust along the way and stay firm. Both his kids were professionals with master's degrees and PhDs, an engineer and a professor at a university. At his age, he would still help them from time to time. Ask yourself, what position would you like to be in your later years?

If you haven't found that desire, that goal, keep searching. It doesn't matter how old you are, or how long it takes you, or even if your friends or family are ahead of you. It's not a race against anyone, it's about you, and you only. Believe me when I tell you that once you find that one thing, you'll find pleasure in executing well over 100 percent effort on it, every single time. You won't find excuses, only an excuse to say "why not." I remember reading about author J.K. Rowling and how she became a writer and how she found the excuse to write every chance she had. She even hand-wrote and used a ten-year-old typewriter. The point is, you don't need to have a new laptop to write. You can start with a piece of paper and a pencil. But you have to decide that you want it, and then take no prisoners, and learn to say "no" to the things that disrupt and interrupt your passion. Build a bunker around that, and let no one get in.

CHAPTER 7

Knowing thyself

IT IS NOT enough to want something, desire something, or need something. While these entities are needed, and often serve as strong drivers toward our goals, they often get stifled. In my line of work, the majority of the clients we serve are traumatized by severe events, or single events that prevent them from recognizing what's five feet in front of them. They live moment to moment because that is what life and circumstances have taught them; or at least what they have been exposed to. This moment-to-moment living lacks forethought to consequences. Thereby, they develop survival skills that prevent them from being hurt or killed. While these are extreme situations, the rest of the population works pretty much in the same manner.

Often officers respond to incidents where inmates, or youths, are highly volatile and aggressive. The client often has no way to communicate, and officers are left with having to control their violent behavior. Once they are de-escalated and have had time to calm down, the conversations take place. Here is what we do; we ask, what happened? We have to pay attention to the root cause of what triggered the outburst, then what action was chosen to deal with the trigger. If you ask these youths what triggered their behavior, they have no clue. So it is the officer's job to draw it out. Officers ask what happened rather than telling them, "What's wrong with you?" To societal standards it is obvious that there is something wrong with the youth. But that is not the issue. The issue is to get the youth to think what the trigger was, what they chose to do about the trigger, and then get them to think of alternatives to deal with their triggers.

Often the mistake officers make is trying to hold a youth accountable to a level of comprehension or expectation much higher than the youth can comprehend or is capable of understanding. It is reasonable to assume that if you've never been taught a coping skill, you can't be expected to exercise that coping skill. You first would've had to be shown it; otherwise your brain has no point of reference to make a sound judgment.

It all made sense to me during a situation with my eight-year-old son. When I picked him from school; he saw me from a distance and quickly smiled and ran toward me. As he approached me, he asked, "Where is Mama?" (His grandmother). He quickly answered his own question and said, "She's at home, right?"

I said, "Yes, why?"

"Oh, because she usually brings me a surprise."

We quickly moved on from that conversation and got inside the car. As we drove home, he seemed excited and eager to get on with his day. We got home, walked up the stairs, and went inside the house. His two-year-old sister greeted him, and so did his grandmother. He then asked, "Mama, where is my surprise?"

My mother said, "You know it is only when I pick you up, and today it was your daddy's turn; you know this."

My son quickly turned his smile into a frown. As we continued to chat and prepare a lunch, we tried to joke with him and play lightheartedly. But everything we said, every laugh was making him cry. When we would ask him what was wrong, he simply shut down, looked down, and cried again. We thought he was being a bit silly with his attitude, so we ignored his behavior and moved on. I then sat down and began to do his homework with him. He was no longer crying, but he was having a hard time understanding the math. He kept getting stuck on concepts that were easy, too easy for him. So what's the deal with this story? Here is the gold nugget, and it happens to us grown-ups often, too many times to count. My son shut down on an event, minuscule to everyone, but it was huge to him. Once he regained composure of himself, he could no longer think, he couldn't problem solve, he couldn't even focus on the simplest of concepts he had already mastered. Ever get stuck like that? So what do we do?

I asked my son, "What's wrong?"

His response was "I don't know" as he frowned again and looked down.

I put down the pencil and told him, "Let's talk

about this. So, if you don't know what's wrong, do you know why you're feeling like this?"

I was met with the same response, "I don't know," as he tried to dig his head under my armpit. "I'm sad."

I pulled him out of my armpit and told him that he wasn't in trouble. So I said, "Let's rewind your day. When I picked you up, did you feel like this?"

He replied, "No."

"When we came up the stairs to the house, did you feel like this?"

"No."

"When you opened the door and saw your sister and your grandma, did you feel like this?"

"No." He then paused, and said, "I got upset when Mama said she didn't have a surprise for me."

This is it, as rudimentary and silly as it sounds, this is the gold nugget. Often we are unable to identify why we feel one way or another, or why we react or act upon an event that triggers our emotional responses. So what do we do if we don't know why? Then you ask "when" and do a walkabout in your mind, leading up to the incident. Do it until you meet that moment in which you went from confident to unsure; do it until you go from happy to sad or anxious. Once you identify when this occurred, you can then ask yourself, *What can I do different? What are my choices?*

Here is the thing; we have to understand that these triggers that prevent you from doing or fulfilling the things you want come from somewhere. And oftentimes they're responses to an external event or series of events that surpass our ability to cope. Therefore, the next time we meet these triggers, we shut down, we run, and as adults we make excuses and justify why things don't go our way. Either we put excessive blame on ourselves or we displace blame, and blame everyone else or the "system." So rather than reacting, we have to learn to do a walkabout in our mind before we go off the deep end. Ask, *Is this a response to a trigger? Am I afraid of this?* Map it out and begin to change the program in your head. See it in your mind so that you can begin to believe it. Once the mind believes, then you'll achieve. Ask any successful person, author, millionaire, athlete, or professional. They have no doubt they are a lawyer or an accountant; they simply know because they believe it. No one has to tell them. So as you are working out the kinks in your belief system, always take time to journal. This is a good practice to later reflect on what was really going through your head. You'll be surprised at the growth you'll be uncovering.

When you finally become aware of yourself, you'll begin to notice what the Nobel Laureate Herbert Simon referred to as "pattern recognition"—basically, the brain's ability to scan our environment, discern order, and create meaning. You'll be able to quickly assess a situation so that you take appropriate action, the right way, at the right time, with a high degree of accuracy. Thus, you'll see opportunity where you couldn't before, and seize it with ease and success. Make no mistake; you have to put in the work. You have to work on getting to know "you" first, know your limits, then work on limit breakers and your growth.

Hacking the pirate's Map

Everyone wants the map, and what better way to attain this map than hacking the pirate's map to the buried treasure. Let's map it all out, but re-member, as you follow this map, do not expect it to do the work for you. This map will not guaran-tee you success, riches, or a cup of coffee. Much like maps on your phone, you have to start driv-ing or walking for the maps to follow you on the GPS. The map then begins to reveal the path. It is up to you to choose which path you want to take and which treasure you want to uncover first. Not all treasures are easily accessible, and some are hidden. Each "golden nugget" is a treasure, and depending where you are in life, you'll need to take steps to acquire them. In some instances you'll only be able to work with what's five feet in front of you. You'll have to trust that the next five feet will reveal more information for you to make a choice. If you treat each five steps like a treasure hunt, and not like a surprise party, you'll find it fun, and you won't be caught off guard. Even if you take a wrong turn, re-route, don't get stuck, and problem solve.

So let me bring this to your doorstep. At the be-ginning of every shift at work, we have what we call "briefings." Sort of like a gathering to talk about issues, fixers, and opportunities to address deficiencies. A meeting of the minds of the sort.

Within a short time of this particular briefing, the team realized that there was a one-hour coverage issue. There was no supervisor on the schedule to cover that one hour. I asked the team if they could talk among themselves and figure out who was going to cover the hour. There was silence; one could drop a pin and hear the echo for miles. One of the sergeants spoke up and said it was his fault for not covering the hour. I interjected and told the group that it was all of our responsibility to ensure the "ship" doesn't sink. That meant that we needed everyone to communicate and extend their best ability to keep the facility running with the adequate coverage to help support line staff. This concept did not compute for one of the supervisors. He spoke up and began to justify that he wasn't going to stay over and that it shouldn't be the expectation to volunteer to stay over their time. He then went on to blame administration for not providing the adequate number of staff to work (a prevailing issue for detention facilities). He very adamantly stated that I would have to "order him" to stay for the hour. The other five supervisors remained quiet. Something strange overcame me. I was not angry, but aroused and bothered by his response and his attitude. I knew that if I let it go, the remaining supervisors' morale would be at stake, as well as the basic respect for the rest of them:

Me: "I'm glad you have the courage to speak up for what other people might be thinking; and since you brought this up, I'll be more than happy to answer your concern. It is not up to administration to solve all of our problems. We can only control what we have in front of us. Do you agree?"

Supervisor: Shrugs his shoulders and nods in agreement.

Me: "Since we can only control what we have here and now, then it is up to us to make sure that the facility has the coverage it needs to support the staff. This can't happen if we are too busy fighting our egos and demand that we have to 'order' people around. While policies and procedures allow me to order you, it is not the type of relationship that I personally want. You know I've worked with you, I trust your judgment, and I've allowed you to work around the obstacles you have. So what makes you think that I need to order you? The bottom line is that we leave this 'leak' in the ship, and tomorrow it will continue to be there, until finally one day, as it is ignored long enough, we all sink."

Supervisor: "But that's what I'm trying to say. Administration doesn't care about the problems we have, nor do they listen to what we have to say. Why don't they come work here for a day and see what we have to do. I shouldn't have to volunteer to stay just because they didn't do their job to staff this place appropriately."

Me: "You are right, I am not going to deny that we have operational issues. But we can't fix that right now. Can you agree that neither you nor I can just go out and hire new people?"

Supervisor: "I can agree with that."

Me: "Since we can't control that part of our environment, what then do we have control over? It's five feet in front of us, that's all we have, here and now; and what's five feet in front of us is our relationship we have with one another. If you want me to write on the Watch Log that I ordered you to stay, then that's all you have to say. It's about communication, and how we communicate this back to our bosses. At the end of the day, our bosses are not here, but we are. Ordering you over to stay an hour only creates animosity and anger—two things I don't want, simply because I wouldn't want that for me either. I've encouraged you and the rest of you to talk to me, in private when it's a personal issue. I have no problem talking openly, but be ready to hear the truth; and the truth is that we only have what's five feet in front of us; what stands in between is what we make of it."

Supervisor: "Yeah, but administration is not on board with any of this."

Me: "It doesn't matter, because the only thing we can control is what we have in front of us. That battle with staffing issues and operational issues requires other people involved, more time, meetings with HR, the chief, and foremost, proposals on how we think improvements can change the quality of our workplace. Tell me this, can you accomplish all this now?"

Supervisor: "No."

Me: "We..." I cleared my throat and paused. "I need your cooperation, not because I'm acting on behalf of administration, but because line staff need you. I need you. And believe it or not, there will be a time when you too will need your staff. No one is an island. We are all interdependent on each other. A lot of things are not under our control, and trying to control them is madness."

Supervisor: Nods in agreement with his head down. "Let our supervisor group talk about who will cover the hour."

Me: "Thanks, I really appreciate that, and I will remember your act of kindness."

At the end of the hour, the supervisor came up and requested to speak to me. We sat down as he began to tell me that he did care about the line staff and his peers. He apologized for his reaction and his perceived selfishness. I thanked him again for speaking up, and rephrased what he told me, allowing him to hear that I heard him. As you can see, there may be plenty examples where even we can't or won't see past five feet in front of us. A map is no guarantee that we will see the path either, but it is better to walk toward the intended direction than to walk in the opposite direction altogether. So how do we hack the pirate's map? Let us trust what we have five feet in front of us, know what we may be coming up with ahead, but worrying about it won't change anything. Know what's ahead and only worry for what you can control five feet in front of you.

Air & Water

A week later I walked into my house to see my son sitting next to my mom. He had his head down, and his body language said he was shut down. I heard my mother tell him about his math, and how behind he was in learning subtraction. I then told my mom to allow a break; he was shut off, and learning requires him to be open. I approached my son and asked him to breathe. He immediately started crying. I asked him to take deep breaths, but he kept crying. Softly I whispered that the body requires two things, air and water. "When you are unable to cope, your body is asking for air and water. Breathe deep, and hold your breath for a second, and then let it out slowly, as slow as possible." My son attempted several times to breathe, but would break and whimper and cry again. "Son, whatever it is that troubles you, it doesn't matter. You'll learn the math anyway, and you're smart. Everything in life is practice, and you just need to be exposed to it more. That's all, it's that easy. But when you keep chopping at it emotionally charged and mentally blocked, no matter how hard you chop, you'll never get anywhere. It's like walking in circles. Step away from what you have, and give your body air and water. You'll see the answers, but you have to trust what you have in front of you, and not worry for what's too far ahead." After several attempts, he finally got the breathing down until he finally calmed himself. With a full glass of water and a few minutes to recollect himself, he finally was able to complete the math. I refrained from saying anything until he said, "Daddy! I got it!"

Begin your work with what's five feet in front of you. While you see it through, there will be no doubt that you will be discouraged, even by the very people who are supposed to help you and encourage you. No need to worry, take a deep breath, several in fact, and take a drink of water, lots of it. If you are unaware of breathing techniques, enroll in classes that teach you. There is a reason why birthing mothers are taught these basic techniques. It helps you cope and to stay in the moment. That is after all what you are trying to do, cope and stay in the moment, stay in the game while "in the zone."

CHAPTER 8

When In Rome

WHEN YOU DO as they do (your models), you'll see patterns and habits reveal themselves to you. You'll have to put your own way of doing things on the back burner for a bit. Once you've adapted, you'll begin to add new "wiring" to your thought process. Meaning, you'll see the meaning for saving, frugality, self-education, journaling, eating right, exercise, and time to self-assess and evaluate. You'll see most if not all patterns emerge, seeing each subsequent trait manifest as a daily habit like the Romans did. So, as the old adage goes, "When in Rome, do as Romans do."

These ancient Roman soldiers guarded their thought process; not for a minute did they allow their mind to think of themselves as anything less than. Therefore, their cultural patronage propelled them for mental dominance, and anything less would be "un-Roman-like." This serves as a comparison to illustrate the process. Taking it to your doorstep, this really means to do as those you wish to become like. If you want to be a great athlete, train like one. If you want to be a writer, write and seek feedback. Once you have enough understanding of what you want, you'll want to seek a "master mind" group (support group), people who think and do as you want to become. Nothing really comes without putting in the work. Small steps toward what you want progressively create the overload you need, each time preparing you to be able to take on heavier, more complex loads. Eventually each small step becomes too fast to stop; like geometric progression you'll be able to topple situations at twice your previous capabilities.

When you finally make a decision to stop making excuses, you'll need to start somewhere. You'll have to make an assessment; an inventory of your strengths and weaknesses. You'll need to make a SWOT analysis of yourself in order to determine what you have. You can't go to war without first understanding if you have enough infantry, weapons, supplies, food, and equipment. The SWOT analysis model simply illustrates strengths, weaknesses, opportunities, and threats. Remember that everything and anything that attacks your comfort zone is a threat, and your psyche will do everything to fight it. Therefore you'll need to come up with strategies to check yourself whenever you start to "fall off the wagon."

If you are deep in emotional turmoil, seek professional help first. You can't un-hoard your "stuff" without first understanding why you're hoarding in the first place. You'll end up hoarding again. Earlier we spoke about cognitive behavioral therapy. If anything else seems too far out for you to believe in or engage with, a widely accepted therapeutic model like this one can benefit you greatly to begin your healing and your journey. Part of your SWOT analysis will help you determine what you want. That could range from an explosive transformation to simply returning to a state of normalcy where you can begin to function without peril, severe anxiety, depression, and so forth.

It took me many years to determine what supplements worked for me, what foods agreed with me, what allergies I had, and how these allergies, foods, and supplements affected me day in and day out. Ignoring the symptoms of food allergies and supplements creates a compound effect in your body and how you interact with the world around you. These can range from constipation, bloating, body aches, acne, obesity, lethargy, etc. None of these symptoms can possibly make you feel great. Sometimes all you need is a small adjustment, but it can be like finding a needle in a haystack. This is why it's imperative to self-assess, evaluate, compare, and foremost, to write it down. After all, you're servicing the most advanced hardware in the planet—, you. Finding the right method is like finding the right person. Just because there might be a perfect person, that doesn't mean they are perfect for you. Likewise the method works very much the same way. It may sound perfect, but it might not be perfect for you. This is why you begin with the process of elimination, with self-evaluation and assessment. You'll have to hack at what works and what doesn't work until you reveal what is perfect for you.

Finally, remember that intention and being in the "here and now" is as important as planning ahead. Some tasks will be too daunting, too complex, or too overwhelming. Therefore planning for ten, even twenty feet ahead, and then focusing on the first five feet ahead of you will help you stay focused. I've been very fortunate to have people in my life to support my focus and my ambitions. It's the tribe members you choose to have around you who will facilitate whatever journey you are seeking. Without your tribe, your process can slow down or speed up. In many cases, as it was for me, it was my son's grandparents, my children, my mother, my wife, friends and collogues who helped bring out the best in me. Today, we share meals together at holidays and extend our gratitude to one another. While the question of my son's mother's whereabouts still remains, there is no doubt that we all wish her the very best. No person should be indebted to the slavery and servitude of addiction. My son, now eight, has no idea where she is or whether he will ever know her. We all have a story to tell, and my son, too, will have to tell his one day. As for now, my job is to continue to develop in him mental fortitude and strength of character so that he may one day face and cope with twice his current capabilities.

Resolve to Live as a Grown-Up

What you want, wants you. When I set out on this journey, I wanted a successful relationship, a home, peace, and happiness. For others it may be one or several, or perhaps material wealth. But not everyone wants what you want or in the same quantities, and this is why abundance is available to everyone. After several marriages, and even more relationships, it dawned on me to ask, "What do I want? Why do I keep being dissatisfied?" As I honed in on this, I realized it was peace and a successful relationship that I wanted. Though sadly, even when I met my wife I still didn't recognize it right away. Realistically, you may not either, and that's okay. However, with self-assessment and evaluation you will quickly see what's in front you, and determine whether what you have in front of you is worth your time and effort. Employing mental walkabouts helps not only identify where you may have lost your composure, but also how you wish to see yourself in the future, like a mental projection. You have to be honest with yourself when you project yourself so that it is somewhere between reality, achievable, measurable, and yet, just out of reach—something you have to work toward— but not too far out that you think it's a myth to achieve. When I finally was able to see my wife interact with my family, I saw her with me. Cliché? Perhaps, but it is necessary to do this.

Now looking in from the outside, it is clear how the progressive overloads created geometric progression. Each time you take a step toward your goals, steadily increasing the demands, your mind, body, and spirit prepare you to take on more. Hence allowing you to handle and topple things past your current limit. Again, to recap, for this to even work you have to decide what you are going to demand of yourself. It could be a multitude of things, ranging from small to big. Keep a journal, as not all things you'll achieve in a short time. When you create this set-up, you are living by design and not by default.

You will always start out with the things you know. Progressive overload puts you just outside that norm, or your state of normalcy. Eventually, these incremental steps will raise your level of belief in yourself, putting you in what you know that you don't know. Meaning, you will enter the realm of possibilities. Each time you forego those possibilities, you'll be taking steps back. This will make you rethink your choices and whether or not you will opt to take that choice again. So understanding what you are giving up each time you choose to not seek your path is key in keeping you focused. Develop a list of what you give up each time you say "yes" to other things, and "no" to your goals and dreams. When you do take a setback, take inventory of it and write potential opportunities that come of it.

To visualize this more accurately, see a circle. Our habits and our comfort zones lie inside this circle. What lies outside of that is the realm of possibilities, the things we don't know that we know could exist. The wheel represents major aspects that constantly need your attention, your environment, your self-assessment, assessment/evaluation of its totality, and execution. You will find yourself at any given moment working on one or more aspects of the circle; remember it is never linear. Depending on where you are headed with a particular aspect of your journey or growth, you will seek to change, adjust, and self-assess different areas of your life. However you map out your growth, each step and the methodology you choose is the compass you have to constantly adjust. With work, you'll move out of your current circle, and expand to the outer one, subsequently making the outer circle your new inner circle.

The Inventory

Taking inventory is not only important to self-assess, but it gives you the chance to look at where there was a breakdown, weaknesses, and opportunities. When you identify these areas, it's important to nourish, rest, and take time to appreciate what has just occurred, even if it is perceived as bad. Should you fail to do this, eventually you will experience what's called the law of diminishing returns, meaning each subsequent step you take while depleted or mentally and emotionally drained will only take you further back. The law of diminishing returns is an economic term used to describe the decreased output of a production process as the amount of a single factor is incrementally increased. The key, however, is that this will occur if all other inputs are held fixed. In this case we are dealing with our "fixed," or lack of expansion of emotional and intellectual comprehension of a given situation. Lacking the ability to stop, rest, assess, and nourish what has been broken down in our process will result in frustration and irritability from lack of positive returns. Eventually you will reach the feeling of giving up or hopelessness. As we increase effort, we must also increase our ability to take on more emotionally and intellectually. We must remain open to constructive criticism, and not fall in the fallacy that we are smarter than everyone else. Only in this way can progressive overload create geometric progression; otherwise, any overload will create a geometric regression; that feeling of spiraling down faster the more we do or move, like quicksand.

So without further ado, here are the top ten items; use them as you wish. Remember that at any moment you can be at any given point; therefore, they should not be used as a step-by-step guide, but rather as a compass:

1. *Assess & Re-evaluate*: As often as possible at first. Then stretch it out as needed. This often is best done journaling, or using a method that keeps record.
2. *Accountability*: Hold yourself accountable for good things and bad things, and let go of them quickly and move on.
3. *Feedback:* Force yourself to accept immediate feedback and reward yourself for things accomplished.
4. *Accept where you are:* This helps you take responsibility of where you want to go. Plan for ten to twenty feet in front of you, and focus on what's five feet ahead of you

(what you can control).

5. *Identify when you are projecting:* It's your "stuff" that you project on others. Your "stuff" is yours and you have to find a way to un-hoard all of it; but not on others.

6. *Hydration, Exercise, & Nutrients:* Consume the right things for you.

7. *Get involved*: Committees, groups, a "master mind," conventions, seminars, read, if possible get a mentor (or several).

8. *Abracadabra*: Be present with the words you utter and likewise guard against negative people who utter negativity. While constructive criticism is well intended, often it crosses boundaries into insults. Know the difference.

9. *Walkabout*: Visualize your walkabouts; a mental projection of how you wish to see yourself executing, doing, acting, speaking, etc. The walkabout can be done physically as well. Very much like walking the floor at a company, a warehouse, or like checking your car for damage. It can also serve as an inspection.

10. *When in Rome, do as Romans do*: If you want to perform like an athlete, train like one.

You'll never meet a strong person with an easy past. Take heed in the lessons from these breathing and living bibliographies and take notes; not on what they are doing, but how they did it when they were at your stage. See and study how they planned it out and how they dealt with the twists and turns in their lives. Pick out the people you wish to become like, and begin to map out your course. Remember that if you are not at their level yet, doing what they do will prove frustrating for you. You'll have to do what they did when they were starting out. Skills you'll learn—it's the attitude and passion that can't always be passed on. That, you'll have to develop on your own.

Remember not to beat yourself up. Educate yourself so that you understand where you are. You may have experienced such traumatic events in your life that they no longer qualify as normal stress responses. Some can achieve complete recovery within a very short time, but results vary. Understand that you could be suffering from a complex post-traumatic stress disorder, which can take your recovery longer. Again, this plan does not replace any care you may be needing from a behavioral mental health professional. Seek help, start somewhere, but whatever you do, start today.